WORKLOADS

This book is the sixth in a series published in association with CEDR

Series Editor: *Robin Lovelock*

Already published:

CHANGING PATTERNS OF MENTAL HEALTH CARE
A case study in the development of local services
Jackie Powell and Robin Lovelock

PARTNERSHIP IN PRACTICE
The Children Act 1989
Edited by Ann Buchanan

DISABILITY: BRITAIN IN EUROPE
An evaluation of UK participation in the HELIOS
programme (1988-1991)
Robin Lovelock and Jackie Powell

THE PROBATION SERVICE AND INFORMATION TECHNOLOGY
David Colombi

VISUAL IMPAIRMENT; SOCIAL SUPPORT
Recent research in context
Robin Lovelock

Forthcoming titles:

LIVING WITH DISFIGUREMENT
Psycho-social implications of being born with a cleft palate
Poppy Nash

EDUCATING FOR SOCIAL WORK: ARGUMENTS FOR OPTIMISM
Edited by Peter Ford and Patrick Hayes

DEMENTIA CARE: KEEPING INTACT AND IN TOUCH
A search for occupational therapy interventions
Cathy Conroy

Workloads

Measurement and management

JOAN ORME

Avebury

Aldershot • Brookfield USA • Hong Kong • Singapore • Sydney

Published by
Avebury
Ashgate Publishing Limited
Gower House
Croft Road
Aldershot
Hants GU11 3HR
England

Ashgate Publishing Company
Old Post Road
Brookfield
Vermont 05036
USA

A CIP catalogue record for this book is available from the British Library

ISBN 1 85628 872 2

Library of Congress Catalog Card Number: 95-80356

Printed and bound in Great Britain by
Ipswich Book Co. Ltd., Ipswich, Suffolk

Contents

CONCLUSION

List of tables

Acknowledgements

This book has been a long time in the preparation, and to those involved in the original research, I give my apologies for the lack of public recognition of the commitment that they gave. I hope that they will recognise that the delay has been important in that the timing of this text has meant that it can address a significant development in the discussion of workload measurement and management.

The original research was commissioned by the National Association of Probation Officers (NAPO) in 1989, and was jointly funded by NAPO and the Faculty of Social Sciences at the University of Southampton. The climate then was one of hope for the probation service. It had been protected from the economic stringencies imposed upon other social work services and attention to workloads was seen as necessary to ensure that the service, which was employing a fully qualified social work staff, could continue to provide the highest professional standards within the criminal justice system.

That climate was to change very rapidly. While official publications (*Crime, Justice and Protecting the Public*, 1990) and the subsequent legislation espoused a commitment to continuing the social work base of the probation service, other activities were more threatening. NAPO at first welcomed the 1992 National Probation Survey as a means of demonstrating that the service was working hard, or was overworked. However it became clear that the results were to be used in a way which was wholly undesirable. The documenting of the work of probation assistant grade and the inclusion of information about workloads in financial management information systems paved the way for the argument that professionally qualified workers were expensive. In a political climate which framed value for money in terms of cost, rather than effectiveness in performing the task, NAPO was being out manoeuvred.

Writing the text commenced at the beginning of 1994. It had been earlier envisaged that the results of the research would be published in report form. The changes in criminal justice legislation in the early 1990s might suggest that the results were somewhat outdated. However, the involvement of the author in the NAPO Information Systems Working Party, which met with the team devising the financial management information system for the probation service, and her involvement in the Home Office National Probation Survey, which contributed data on workloads for that information system, made her aware of the potential changes that were being introduced. Work on reviewing the impact of care management on local authority social services confirmed that these changes were taking place not just in the probation service, but throughout the statutory personal social services. However, even access to such an overview did not provide adequate preparation for the scale of the changes in the probation service which have been proposed in the last twelve months.

In a criminal justice system which has abandoned the rehabilitative ideal, a fully qualified probation service, which incorporates a social work value base, is more than an expensive luxury. It is an embarrassment, reminding society that it is not just individual offenders who are responsible for their actions; and that punishment is not the only effective way of deterring criminal behaviour. A two fold attack involved the Dews' Report which has argued against the need for qualifying education and training in an objective and critical environment, that of higher education institutions, and proposed legislation to abandon the very activity which the probation service does best, supervising offenders in the community using the strength of the relationship between worker and offender (*Strengthening Punishment in the Community: a consultation document*, 1995).

At the same time, social workers in the public sector have demonstrated that the pressures that they are under have been exacerbated by a management failure to provide the necessary support and protection. The decision of an Industrial Tribunal in 1994 to uphold the claim of John Walker, a social worker from Northumbria, that repeated mental health problems were caused by the agency's failure to give appropriate workload relief, was a significant milestone. It highlights that stress can have devastating effects for the individual, with equally negative effects on the organisation which loses the services of an employee through sickness absences. However the trend in the 1990s is to uphold a style of management which emphasises the individual's responsibility to cope with whatever workload is allocated. Such practices are, to some extent, imposed upon organisations in the private sector by economic pressures. In the public sector the emphasis on value for money, more often equated with the slogan 'more for less', means that managers have little choice but to demand more of front line workers. The threat to public sector social services is heightened by the introduction of the ideology of the market into welfare services. If public sector agencies cannot produce economic services, then the services will be contracted out to private organisations who can. The threat is therefore to the profession of social work.

The text is significantly different from the original expectation of a research report which would be used in negotiations about time per task and workload limitation in the probation service. It now documents a crucial period in the history of social work in general, and the probation service in particular.

Despite these changes, or perhaps because of them, I am even more indebted to the two probation teams who participated in the original research, and to the offenders on whom they wrote their reports. As well as providing part of the funding, NAPO has been an invaluable source of support. Colleagues on the Information Systems Working Party were generous with their ideas, and Pete Bowyer, Research and Information Officer, assisted in negotiating access, and was always ready to debate a point. However, in acknowledging the support of NAPO, it is important to stress that the ideas in this text are those of the author, and do not represent NAPO policy, although there may be some congruence.

The Faculty of Social Sciences at the University of Southampton also provided part of the funding, and colleagues have contributed ideas in all sorts of ways. Specific thanks are due to Robin Lovelock of CEDR who encouraged the original idea of the text, and gave regular feedback. To the very end he assisted in the presentation of the copy material, but having said that, any errors that remain are wholly the responsibility of the author.

Joan Orme
Department of Social Work Studies
University of Southampton

April, 1995

The author

Joan Orme is a Senior Lecturer in the Department of Social Work Studies at the University of Southampton. Having qualified as a probation officer in 1970 she worked for the Sheffield, Southampton and Hampshire Probation Services before taking up a post as Lecturer at the University of Southampton. Throughout her lecturing career she has maintained an interest in, and commitment to, the probation service and has been an active member of the National Association of Probation Officers (NAPO). For the last decade she has been writing and researching in the area of workloads. Her interest in this comes directly from a belief that the codes and conditions of workers directly affects the quality of the service that they give to users and clients. She has been a member of the NAPO Information Systems Working Group, and between 1989 and 1991 was member of the Home Office National Probation Survey Working Group.

Introduction

It is the contention of this text that whatever the future task or direction of social work intervention it is not possible to proceed without some consideration of the consequences for the individuals who are required to carry out the function of the agency. Whether reviewing the impact of policy decisions related to client groups, or professional decisions about methods of social work practice or intervention, there are implications for workloads of front line social workers.

The notion of workload is in itself complex and below there is an attempt to give a working definition of what is meant by the use of the term in this text. Significantly, the distinction between measurement and management cannot be answered by a simple definition, and it is this which is explored in the body of the text. Drawing on a programme of published and unpublished research, there is an attempt to assess the contribution that workload measurement schemes have made to the decision making processes in social work organisations. The work was undertaken primarily with the probation service, which, at the time of the research, was identified very clearly as a social work agency within the criminal justice service. As has been described in the Acknowledgements that definition was being questioned at the time the text was being prepared.

That very questioning, or more particularly, the way in which a political ideology can bring about dramatic changes in the organisation and delivery of services, has emerged as an important outcome of the study of workloads. Such changes are not unique to the probation service. The

Griffiths Report (1988) and the subsequent legislation (*National Health Service and Community Care Act*, 1990) raised similar considerations for the delivery of community care services by local authority social service departments (Orme and Glastonbury, 1993). Here the issues are about activities of front line social workers, but more particularly, in a policy which advocates a mixed economy of care, the cost of the delivery of services by agencies outside of the statutory sector. Concerns about contracting out and costing services are not only the prerogative of local authority social services department. The *Criminal Justice Act*, 1991, in requiring probation services to enter into partnerships with voluntary and independent sector organisations, introduces the notion of purchasing into the probation service.

Equating workloads with cost is not unusual in some professions. The legal profession charges for its service on the basis of time spent on any particular activity. However, it constitutes a significant development for welfare organisations and adds a further dimension to the study of workloads which has traditionally been associated with allocation of resources on the basis of assessment of need (Coulshed, 1990), or with concerns about stress levels and performance of workers (Vickery, 1977). These issues will be explored again, both in this chapter and towards the end of the text, when more detailed consideration has been given to the process of measuring workloads. However, before proceeding, a clarification of terms is required.

Definitions

Workload

Glastonbury et al (1987) make a clear distinction between the term caseload, which refers to the total number of cases for a single worker, and workload which is the caseload **plus** a number of other activities. These can include tasks which involve working with clients or users of services, such as office duty or intake work, groupwork with users not on an individual worker's caseload, or activities related to work with clients or users which does not involve direct contact, such as travelling and case recording. Additionally there are activities in which front line workers are involved which are not associated with direct client work, but nevertheless contribute to the service offered. Liaison with other organisations and services, supervision of staff by managers, staff training and development are some examples of these activities.

The distinction between workload and caseload is therefore a significant one, especially for front line workers. A comprehensive definition of workload can offer some protection both, in the allocation of work and in the assessment of performance. If either is undertaken merely on the basis

2

of the number of cases that are being carried, rather than acknowledging the range of tasks being undertaken on behalf of the agency, the worker may be over burdened, or assessed unrealistically. The notion of workload also underlines the range of activities undertaken by social workers, and the skills required. Any workload audit reveals that social work is a complex and multi-faceted activity (BASW, 1977, Barclay, 1982).

Workload measurement

The definition of workload is further complicated by an acknowledgement that the various activities do not carry equal weight. Differences occur between activities. For example, how does a morning's duty equate to supervision of a child abuse case? There are also different patterns of demand within categories of work, in that the expectation of contact will vary depending upon the demands or needs of the case. A 'supervision' case may be of a highly volatile family situation, or it may involve on-going support for a chronic situation. This acknowledgement of different needs and different patterns of work has opened up a debate about differential weightings for activities or interventions. It is the attempt to reflect these differences that has led to the notion of workload measurement.

Workload measurement can therefore be used to refine the allocation of work (including specific cases) to ensure equity between workers. In helping to identify demand it can also assist managers deploy staff according to activities, or even geographic regions. However, in helping to resolve some problems, workload measurement raises many more. The first is identifying a unit of measurement which can be used to reflect the demands of the work in a particular agency. The second is how to achieve an accurate reflection of the work demands to ensure comparability. If workload measurement is important for the protection of workers and the deployment of resources, how is workload measured?

It is in this latter area that research has made a significant contribution. However, in doing so, it has raised further complexities, as the rest of this text explores.

Workload management

Workload management occurs at a number of levels. All workers manage their work to a greater or lesser extent, by diary recording and a series of decisions about when and how to perform tasks (Coulshed, 1990). At an organisational level, it involves systematic handling of cases and other components of the workload. This handling can, or should, include an evaluation (usually a weighting) of the various pieces of work to enable them to be related to a workload ceiling or working week, a further evaluation (qualitative) to check the balance of the workload and its fit

3

with the skills and interests of the worker. Ideally this management is supported by a supervisory process which tracks a piece of work from start to finish.

The implications of the above process are that a front line manager (or a self-managing senior practitioner or outposted worker) has to make decisions about rationing and prioritising work. This involves additional tasks including scrutinising referrals, giving them a priority rating, allocating them to staff, balancing the workloads of a team, and operating a routine to deal with emergencies or important work which arrives at a time when all staff are functioning at the workload ceiling (Glastonbury et al, 1987).

Hence, workload management has to take place within a whole range of activities which include staff supervision, appraisal and staff development. These occur at the interface of managers and front line workers. Workload management also has implications for the most senior managers who, on the basis of monitoring and auditing activities, will have to make decisions about prioritising, rationing and ultimately withdrawing a service. In recent debates about the organisation of social services these latter activities have become integrally linked with cost, or more particularly 'value for money' (Audit Commission, 1986 and 1989). As such they have focused not only on whether a service is provided, but also on who performs that service (Griffiths, 1988; Audit Commission, 1986).

Rationale

The objectives of a comprehensive workload management system, based on some form of measurement, include ensuring that the best available service is offered to needy clients, operating a fair rationing process when that is necessary, seeking service approaches which maximise cost-effectiveness, protecting and developing staff by confirming that they have a suitable workload both in nature and volume, and keeping the turnover of work on as even a path as possible.

For both the professional worker and the front line manager there is a continuous process of comparing the importance and progress of this sequence between different cases and with other kinds of work. If pressures from elsewhere become too intense, then delaying or postponement devices have to come into play: if pressures ease then processes can be speeded up or other tasks taken on. All of these activities require judgement and information. The judgement is professional and managerial, to ensure that basic objectives are not lost. It is important to keep in mind that these workloads are not being managed in a haven of tranquillity with plenty of time for reflection, but in the hiatus of an office being bombarded with demands which are neither evenly phased nor predictable. The information required is detailed up-to-date material about clients and resources. Often it is needed very quickly, especially if there are any risk factors that need to be picked out. With the development of information technology and its increasing availability in social work agencies, such information can be readily available on screen in response to a few keyboard strokes (Colombi, 1994).

There are other benefits from the output of a workload management system. The process of measurement enhances the ease with which the state of needs (or demands) and resources can be communicated, whether to senior managers or to those who make political decisions. Those same measurements are also valuable planning tools in relation to future staffing levels, and the appropriate focus of staff development and training. In the context of care management such measurements become essential to the whole process of creating, pricing and delivering packages of care (Orme & Glastonbury, 1993).

The tools for coping with high levels of need are familiar to social workers, and operate outside a formal workload management system. But too often in these circumstances they operate as unregulated pressures, putting staff under stress, because they are not based on the essentials of measured needs and monitored workloads. Despite the studies documented in the next chapter, few agencies use anything more than a rule of thumb approach in estimating the scale of the task involved in meeting a given need, though it has to be accepted that more sophisticated measurements do present a difficult challenge. Yet the much easier job of monitoring an individual's workload is also widely shirked

Stress

Social workers experience stress. A profession which deals with other people's emotional problems is bound to reflect and absorb the tensions which clients bring. Pritchard (1985) identifies special features of social service departments which create and intensify the stress experienced by staff. These include the 'risk' element involved in significant decisions and exposure to public hostility, or more accurately 'antagonistic demands' (1985, p7). In addition all occupations which have no control over the demands made of them experience levels of stress. In social work this lack of control relates to the difficulty in anticipating level of demand, but it also reflects a continuing tension about the level of involvement social workers should have, and whether social work is to be governed by the needs of clients, or the resources that are available. To give a simple answer to this latter problem does not resolve the social workers dilemma. Offering a resource led service can lead to increased demands on social workers to explain and justify rationing processes, and to work with those whose needs cannot be met in finding other resources, or coming to terms with the deficit. The consequences of such pressures are manifest in identified patterns of behaviour, including de-energising, reification, burnout and the cycle of chaotic practice (Vickery, 1977; Cherniss, 1980)), all of which affect the quality of the service offered to individual users of the service, and ultimately affect output in that the level of functioning of individual workers may be severely reduced, either by low levels of activity or by periods of absence due to stress related illness.

Context

For these reasons social work has, since its inception, tried to make some sense of the demands. In the last century, the Charity Organisation Society workers were encouraged to keep lists of their cases, as were the forerunners to the probation service, the Police Court Missionaries. As well as the positive reasons for seeing what was being done, there were issues of accountability, even before social workers were paid and before the introduction of performance indicators.

Interest in workloads in the social work profession has occurred in two main waves, if it can be assumed that journal articles and text books reflect professional interest. In the early 1970s the work of the National Institute of Social Work (NISW) around case review and case management was part of a range of activity in Britain and the United States. The timing of this interest is not insignificant, coinciding in Britain with the creation of local authority social services departments as a result of the Seebohm report (HMSO, 1969). The aim of this work was to bring order out of chaos and this was integrally linked to the development of a social work profession. The expansion of the social services post Seebohm also led to calls for 'greater public accountability of social services and social work activities which, until fairly recent times, were considered to be private transactions carried out in one-to-one relationship behind closed doors' (Goldberg & Fruin, 1976, p4). The schemes developed were based on what was actually done with individual clients and were framed around intervention in each case.

Hence Parsloe (1981) identified that all the teams studied in her research had procedures for receiving work into the agencies and for allocating it between workers. Significantly, what was lacking was shared criteria for who should do what in the team; the kinds and amount of work members should undertake. She comments that 'they lacked common instruments for assessment, work planning, work allocation and case and workload management' (1981, p60). Having reviewed the extant schemes at the time, her conclusions were that workload instruments which did exist did not provide easy answers. That there had been no analysis of whether designing such instruments had been useful to workers may be the reason for the lack of enthusiasm for schemes in agencies, and lack of attention to this subject in social work literature for the next decade.

The resurgence of interest in workloads was again precipitated by a challenge, or more accurately a threat, to the social work profession. In 1980 the incoming government commissioned a review of social work. The Barclay Report (1982), which was the product of the review, made some clear statements about the role and tasks of social workers, although the minority reports reflect a lack of consensus. While the recommendations of the Barclay Report were never implemented as a package they have been mediated through a series of reports e.g. Griffiths (1988) and Wagner (1988), finally coming to fruition in the white paper *Caring for People* (1989). The activity of reframing the social work task was paralleled by an equally important review of the performance of the social work profession. Through a series of Audit Commission reports (1986; 1989), and the development of performance indicators (Home Office, 1988), employers and employees were being held to task, without any clear agreement or clarification of what that task was.

The notion of what tasks have to be performed, and how much work can be done in a given period of time, is fundamental to workload management schemes. Such calculations can be inexorably linked to staffing levels, which in turn affect the performance of workers. They are also used in assessment of performance and indicators of throughput or efficiency. The application of workload measures in such contexts serve to put pressure on social work staff, who already experience stress levels related to the nature of their work.

Workloads and stress

In 1988 a survey was commissioned by the National Association of Local Government Officers (NALGO), the trade union for social work staff, to assess whether staff vacancies contributed significantly to stress experienced by workers in local authority social service departments. The findings that only 43% of a sample of 177 social workers were part of a workload measurement scheme (Hayes et al, 1989) were significant in that the research found a direct correlation between the existence of workload schemes and levels of stress. Workers with high stress levels being twice as likely to have no workload review or measurement as those with low stress (Hayes et al, 1989, p41). Without measurement there can be no accuracy. Without accuracy there can be no clearly identified workload ceiling for staff, and without a protected ceiling the pressure of needs is transferred directly to front line staff with consequent impacts on stress, capacity to cope and morale. Workload management is a system designed to make best use of staff and other resources; it is also a system to protect staff from exploitation. As confirmation of this, the NALGO study (Hayes et al, 1989) found that social worker stress was not due so much to the intrinsic nature of the task itself, but to increasing and largely uncontrolled level of demand, and the inability of local management to do anything about it because of inadequate resourcing (1989, p47). What was described as a 'coping culture' emerged, but it was recognised that this involved skipping some tasks while prioritising others, but not in any managed way.

The experiences of social workers are linked, according to Payne (1979), to the need for attention to three underlying themes: demand, constraints and support, to ensure organisational and emotional health. When these themes were examined in the NALGO study (Hayes et al, 1989) it was found that lack of resources, volume of work and pressures from client need were the dominant causes of stress among local authority social services workers. Pritchard (1985) also identified the need for an appropriate level of staff development and training, but this has to be accompanied by managerial support, which can manifest itself in all sorts of ways. One such form of support is the introduction of workload management systems, but not as an end in themselves. In concluding that the most helpful system of workload management involved a common departmental framework with attention to local situations, Pritchard (1985) acknowledges that they can facilitate a bridge between operational needs and staff development and training.

Furthermore, Pritchard's findings (1985), that satisfaction resulted from **positive** work with clients and the exercise of **successful** professional responsibilities has implications for workload measurement and management. The opportunity to have a positive outcome of either an interaction with a client, or from the undertaking of a professional task is often, but not always, linked to having an appropriate amount of time to undertake the task, without being pressured by competing demands. A further significant pre-requisite, as the NALGO study (Hayes et al, 1989) demonstrated, is access to the appropriate resources. This mirrored Pritchard's findings that a common source of dissatisfaction was 'insufficient time and resources for clients' (1985, p37).

Workloads and rationing

Workload measurement in itself cannot produce more time or bring about successful intervention. Workload management can contribute to this, but has to encompass a set of decisions or activities which at first glance appear to be alien to the social work profession. Rationing, the limiting of services to clients, is one example of this. The suggestion that services would not be offered to some clients or that they be limited, has resonance with notions of deserving and undeserving, or an even more random systems of first come first served. Rationing has occurred in social work, but not always openly as Vickery acknowledges, 'many of these rationing devices are covert, working against an agency's expressed aim to help the people who are in greatest need of the particular services it has to offer' (1977, p3).

The debate about procedures for rationing, conducted according to

8

publicly agreed criteria, had been raised in earlier discussions about workload (Parker, 1967; Algie, 1971). Formal rationing could be achieved by limiting the number who are informed of the availability of services, narrowly defining eligibility, making procedures difficult and off putting, or by a system of waiting lists. This was seen as preferable to rationing by an individual social worker of the many high priority cases on a random and ad hoc basis which was blatantly unfair, led to a dilution of service and created chaos in the management of caseloads. It also contributed to the 'cycle of chaotic practice' with a contingent 'failure to make adequate assessment and review of cases and to use the best possible methods, as with too large caseloads and a failure to plan to best advantage' (Vickery, 1977 p5).

Part of the reason for the informality and chaos has been a reluctance on the part of social workers to accept the principles of overt rationing, perceiving it as in some way counter to the ethical base of social work which was formed around notions of acceptance. However Glastonbury is quite clear about the need for such a system, 'there seems to be little doubt that most social services departments are obliged to ration their services, and that the extent of rationing has increased as financial stringency and inflation have put a brake on budgetary growth' (1979, p90). This is part of the dilemma. Ideally, social work would like to operate a fully resourced service, with the capacity to meet needs. Political imperatives, however, highlight the crucial debate about the role of social work and whether a needs led or resource led service is appropriate or feasible, given the economic climate.

However some analysts (Knapp, 1984) regret that social administrators have only turned to a careful examination of costs at a time of economic adversity. It is argued that there has been a lack selectivity in the information considered about costs of services, 'staffing ratios have been criticised for wasting valuable skilled resources, community resources have been exploited with little regard for their effectiveness, maintenance expenditure has been greatly reduced, and new capital projects have been pruned and/or postponed. The sad fact about a lot of this well meant activity is that it is misplaced and misdirected' (Knapp, 1984, p50). Such misdirected activity has influenced workloads carried by individual workers, as well as the organisation of service delivery. A systematic and consistent approach to workload measurement and management might avoid the knee jerk reaction described by Knapp.

Furthermore, as long as the basis of rationing is determined by circumstances outside the immediate control of the agency, then social workers will have little control over their own professional lives. While it is accepted that priority must go to servicing statutory needs and emergencies, it is also likely that even this level of demand could be too much for the workforce. The detailed decisions that occur at point of referral will be transferred to area team level, or to an even more distant

9

point in the organisation. Such lack of control over decision making contributes to worker stress, especially among middle managers (Pritchard, 1985).

Workloads and costs

Rationing of services, allocation of cases and organisation of service delivery are all integrally associated with costs. The simple cost calculations are based on the amount it costs to employ a particular worker to perform a particular task within the organisation, including all the oncosts which are needed for the infrastructure. While Knapp (1984) undertakes a seemingly comprehensive analysis of the cost of social care, distinguishing between accounting costs and opportunity costs, he makes little reference to the supply of social worker input. In global terms he identifies staff wages, availability and turnover as contributing to the input costs of the provision of labour. That costs are further influenced by how many tasks staff members perform, or how many cases they carry is seemingly ignored. The need to measure workloads to identify costs, or to manage them to influence costs is not discussed.

Social worker activity is discussed only tangentially in an analysis that the cost of a service cannot be reckoned merely by reference to its price, but must be gauged by what is given up, the opportunity cost which could include what other tasks a social worker could be performing (Knapp, 1984, p111). For the purposes of studying workloads, it could be argued that the cost of a social worker sitting in court all morning for a five minute hearing includes the value of the worker's time which could have been spent in alternative activities. Such considerations have led to questions about appropriate activities for professionally qualified social workers, who are the agency's most expensive resource.

If it is not necessary for a qualified social worker to carry out all social care and social welfare tasks, then who should perform them? Local authority social services departments have never had a fully qualified workforce and have used unqualified workers in a number of tasks, many of them involving direct contact with clients or users. The probation service, while having a fully qualified staff, has employed an ancillary or assistant grade to provide support functions, some of which include direct work with clients. Such grades are fully paid employees of the service, albeit on low salaries.

In a prophetic anticipation of the commissioning activities under community care policies, Glastonbury observes that 'it would be an important development if social services departments knew those areas of need where they must direct their own resources, and those areas where they can anticipate a dependable voluntary effort' (1979, p90). In the arrangements for community care (Department of Health, 1989) the concept of statutory organisations purchasing services provided by the voluntary and independent sector (the purchaser/provider split) is integrally linked to notions of cost (Audit Commission, 1986).

Such arrangements present a threat to professional practitioners, because they require an analysis of the skills (or competencies) to perform the task, decisions about who should acquire those skills, and to what level of expertise. The apparent erosion of the professional social work task by the use of volunteers, unqualified workers or workers from other care sectors i.e. health, has led to understandable distrust of current policy initiatives, and of the involvement of organisations such as the Audit Commission or management consultants in reviews of social work provision. The notion of contracting and commissioning carries with it implications for workloads. To contract, and subsequently cost, a service there needs to be an analysis of the input, which includes worker time. As was illustrated above, such a process is a regular activity for some professionals, such as lawyers.

Current concerns

This distrust has precipitated a third wave of interest in workloads, the notions of economy, efficiency and effectiveness being at the root of the discussions. Economy has been equated to the cheapest means of producing the service, which usually assumes that this provision will come from outside the statutory sector, with an emphasis on developing the independent sector. The operation of quasi-markets assumes that introducing a competition between providers of services will produce cheaper alternatives. Such calculations require careful consideration to ensure that the comparisons are equitable. So the full cost of commissioning and purchasing services under packages of care for community care arrangements demand a full audit of workloads of all those involved to ensure that full costs are calculated (Orme, 1993).

The notion of efficiency has direct implications for the study of workloads in that it is usually assumed to be achieved when more work is undertaken by the same number of workers, either by performing more tasks, or by completing tasks more quickly. Hence response times reflected in the community care planning process and national standards for probation (1992) become the yardstick of efficiency and quality. What is not included in this calculation is any notion of preventative work. It may be more efficient to offer a service at an early stage, to avoid more substantial costs at a later stage (Hadley and McGrath, 1980).

Efficiency therefore cannot be separated from considerations of effectiveness, and whether the service offered achieves the best outcome. A discussion of the best outcome involves evaluation of the service offered from the perspective of all concerned: the recipient, the worker, the agency, policy makers and the tax paying public who pay for the service. For the

11

purposes of this text the discussion focuses on the activity of the worker, and whether workload measurement and management allow for the best possible professional practice to be achieved in any given situation.

Conclusion

In this introduction there has been an attempt to set out some of the reasons for studying workloads. Working definitions of terms have been offered, and themes as diverse as worker stress and economic analysis of social care have been introduced to illustrate the centrality of workload measurement and management in the organisation of the delivery of social services. This organisation involves management, not in a narrow sense, but in a broad context which includes decisions about who should be seen by social workers, and what kind of intervention should be undertaken. The way that workload schemes have impinged upon what are otherwise seen as professional decisions is discussed in Chapter One.

Chapter 2 explores the significance, but also the complexity, of researching the social work task, exploring one particular social work intervention for the purposes of studying workload measurement. Attention is paid to the resistance of practitioners to research into social work. This is followed in Chapters 3, 4 and 5 by the description of a particular research project which was funded by the National Association of Probation Officers (NAPO). This project was part of ongoing work which highlights the practical limitations of workload measurement schemes and addresses the political context of such schemes. In particular, the critique of existing schemes is that they measure tasks, but that the measurements are not related to the standard of work undertaken. The linking of notional times to activity has implications for who does the work, as well as the amount of work that has to be done. Chapter 6 discusses the implications of the findings for the probation service, focusing on the role and function of front line managers. Finally, Chapter 7 addresses the significant changes in service delivery which have occurred in both probation and local authority social services, including arrangements for contracting out services. The consequences of these changes mean that workload measurement has become a political issue, central to the introduction of management information systems into social work agencies. The implications of this for service delivery, for the workloads of social workers and for the future of social work are discussed.

1 Workload measurement

Introduction

Workload schemes began to be codified in the early 1970s. An overview of existing methods of measuring workloads reveals a division between those which attempt a level of precision, and the more arbitrary measures. A systematic analysis of sample workload schemes to date helps to clarify the complexities of measurement. Each scheme has a positive contribution to make to the development of systems to help ensure that work is allocated equitably and appropriately, but each has its limitations. Also, starting from the premise that social work will always be in a position where demand exceeds supply, it is possible to identify how the emerging workload measurement schemes have contributed to discussions about workload ceilings, rationing and prioritising, as well as the allocation of the work.

The aim here is not to argue for an 'expert system' of workload measurement, the central thesis of this text is that such a goal is not achievable. The contention is that researching workloads contributes to the body of knowledge about what social workers do, how they spend their time. In understanding this, consideration can be given to how the process can be managed so that the greatest benefits can accrue to those who provide services, as well as those who receive them. In describing and analysing workload schemes, this chapter will clarify the parameters of a research project which attempted to address an aspect of workload measurement which had not, to that point, been addressed, which was linking measurement with good practice.

Workload measurement models

Over the past two decades the attention to workloads which has been documented in the previous chapter has led to a number of emergent models. These reflect some of the tensions which arise when developing systems to measure and manage workloads. In documenting the schemes below it becomes clear that the greatest tension is between worker autonomy and accountability. Schemes which attempt to capture the demands of individual cases on the worker of necessity require information about professional decisions such as frequency of contact or assessment of risk. Systems for acquiring this information can be experienced as inspectorial or challenging the individual worker's decision making. Alternatively, schemes which taker a broader approach, classifying activities or tasks for the purpose of allocation are criticised for not reflecting the volatility of caseloads.

A further tension relates to how the workload system is introduced, whether it is at the request of front-line workers or managers. Schemes which are worker generated often reflect the need to protect workloads, to enable the best working conditions which will enhance the quality of service to those clients and users who are in receipt. Management generated schemes may wish to aggregate data to argue for more resources. More pragmatically, they may be required to ensure service efficiency, which include ways of offering services to a greater number of users and services. Ultimately, both approaches are concerned about conditions of service for workers and quality of services to users. A further dimension is when the schemes developed are a result of collaboration of front line workers and managers with independent researchers.

Case review system

This system was developed as part of an action research programme undertaken by Goldberg and Fruin who attempted 'the elucidation of operational principles which determine the allocation and use of manpower (sic), professional skills and other resources to meet different types of client need' (1976, p10). A review of cases was undertaken with practitioners in which they were encouraged to evaluate their aims with particular cases, and be more explicit about both the ends and means of their activities. During this action research it became apparent that an ongoing case review mechanism would be helpful to practitioners. It would also enhance the quality of service to clients by enabling social workers to plan and evaluate their work with clients, assist the process of supervision

14

and be used as a management tool for planning services. As such it attempted to acknowledge the competing demands on workload measurement systems.

The ensuing case review system attempted to monitor case management from the start, with its emphasis on turnover and productivity, and compared plans with achievements. It involved a form (part of which was pre-coded) which consisted of three sections: past activities; present situation and intended future activities and aims. Hence information about current activities could be used to make some predictions about likely levels of future activity. The data collected could provide information for practice, education and research. As an information system in its own right it gave an 'on-going account of the size, nature and scope of social work activities with different client groups' (Goldberg and Fruin, 1976 p16).

A contentious area was the evaluation of those cases for which productivity and turnover are meaningless terms. These included the 'huge static caseloads of elderly and disabled clients (which) aroused much discussion among the workers, some claiming that persons on the disabled register could never be "closed" ' (Goldberg & Fruin, 1976 p13). The tension around this body of work was resolved by the development of an 'agency caseload' of cases which only needed occasional surveillance for indefinite periods, thus freeing the social workers from the stifling effects of over-large caseloads.

Significantly, the case review system provided much information and patterns of work were discernible, but although some predictive measures were built in, the system was still essentially retrospective and descriptive. The research team implementing the system was asked to weight different types of cases according to the resources, social work time, skills and services to enable managers to allocate cases on a more rational basis and to ensure reasonably balanced caseloads. However, subsequent analysis tended to concentrate on the descriptive profile of the cases and the nature of social work intervention, rather than developing a proactive management system, although it provided information about productivity and turnover. The weaknesses of this system are that workload ceilings are not identified and, other than the development of the 'agency caseload', there is no attempt to establish priorities. While Parsloe (1981) describes the scheme as being useful in helping teams to process work and classify clients, an identified weakness is that it focused solely on work with cases and did not reflect work not directly linked to individual cases. Additionally, in concentrating on social work intervention, it did not necessarily capture all the activity relating to cases. For example, administrative tasks, record keeping and travel, all of which are time consuming and add to the demands on social workers, were not included. It did, however, provide an evaluation of actual work undertaken against assessment, which could provide some measure of effectiveness.

In a further analysis of the tension between models of workload monitoring introduced by management and those supported by front line workers, Vickery (1977) argued that top down solutions transfer conflicts and pressures down the organisational hierarchy, to the interface between client and social worker. It is at this point that decisions about intervention, or non-intervention, are made. How to make these decisions, how to resolve conflict and how to solve problems should therefore include bottom up solutions. Attention must be paid to the circumstances in which the problem resolution occurs in order to ensure that positive adaptations occur, rather than maladaptations. The consequences of this are that 'if successful, change at the field level impinges on the agency's practice at the administrative and policy level' (1977, p7). Alternatively, unsuccessful change can lead to poor service, stressed workers and risks, at best, poor practice and, at worst, tragedy. Initial organisational responses to demands on resources focus at the individual level, either on the individual worker's performance or on problematic caseloads. Solutions include asking individuals to do more, either by a straight allocation of more cases or by evolving new methods of work which, by doing things differently, mean that workers do more. The introduction of intake teams who adopted the principles of task centred casework for organisational reasons are an example of this (Buckle, 1981). Such solutions fail to take a holistic view of agency practice, incorporating all its activities. Vickery (1977) therefore proposed that all activities of the worker be considered in any measurement scheme, thus acknowledging total workload and the way it impinges on availability of time to deal with caseload. Her scheme involved a three stage process.

The first stage addressed the problem of assessment and intervention planning, acknowledging that, at times, even cruder means are used to identify work to be done. A review of existing caseloads, including the criteria for opening, continuing and closing cases was undertaken by the social worker *with* supervisor/manager and an analysis of reasons for intervention based on client problem undertaken. The use of problems as a criterion became contentious when making decisions about closure. Often there were continuing problems not being solved by social work intervention which should not be the focus of social work attention.

Some of these equated to the intractable cases identified in Goldberg and Fruin's study (1976) as the agency caseload. Others highlighted that, at times, the nature of work undertaken limits social worker activity, or the rights of the client. In identifying the need to distinguish between services provided directly (e.g. respite care and emotional support), and those that might be better provided elsewhere, Vickery (1977) was anticipating policy decisions which were incorporated into the principles of care management.

A recommendation that identified problems be aggregated so that needs could be met by other resources in the agency, which might involve a different use of time (e.g. groupwork, community support) has implications for accounting of worker activity. Fundamental to devising schemes for workload measurement is whether the measurement is of individual worker activity or total input to individual cases. Often the decision about how work is captured relates to the purpose of the workload scheme. Those which have a primary aim of protecting workers will concentrate on individual worker activity. Those which argue for increased resources attempt to capture all input into cases from any source within the agency.

The second stage of the case review system involved scanning records of assessments and plans for intervention. This process assumed that clear statements of agreements (or lack of agreements) are needed to establish goals and the resources needed to achieve them (Vickery, 1977). The measurement involved recording frequency of contact needed with client and/or other person in relation to the goals to be achieved, and is described by Vickery as one of the key areas linking the assessment/planning statement to management of social workers' time (1977, p27). However, in attempting to devise a scheme which was not totally reactive to client need, she acknowledges that it is also important to document 'time needed for work that is not direct contact with client/s or others' (1977, p36).

The third stage required a diary exercise to plot time needed to meet demands of a given group of clients. Often there is not enough time available to meet all the demands, and decisions have to be made by supervisors with workers, and preferably with senior management in the agency, about which cases will be given lowest priority and taken off the worker's caseload. Recording of actual work is then used to give a picture of how workable that caseload is.

Despite this detailed analysis of need, Vickery rejects the notion of weighting cases, which would equate to a form of measurement. She suggests that weightings might constrain workers' allocation of time and that the scheme would be less responsive to client need. However, in reviewing the application of the scheme, she acknowledges that there is the possibility of aggregating data which could be used to identify patterns of contact, and even identify predictive factors. This potential has meant that, although staff intensive, the scheme has been used as the basis for other systems.

The limitations of Vickery's scheme are that it has limited potential to ration or limit workloads. This is primarily because, although non-client work is acknowledged, the focus is on work with cases. Workers who appreciate the scheme are usually well organised, presumably because they record frequently and appropriately and have the information on which decisions can be made. Ironically, it is those workers who do not behave in this way, those who are in Vickery's 'circle of chaotic practice' (1977),

17

who might well require help in organising their workload. Finally, the system has been criticised for being both labour and time intensive for both worker and supervisor, and as such counter productive in terms of workload pressure.

Vickery's system is geared to making decisions about best professional practice and, although the need for cut off is identified, the main purpose of the scheme is to ensure that the organisation is geared to offering the best service to the client. As such it gives limited protection to the worker. Furthermore the close involvement of the supervisor/manager in decisions about intervention may present a direct challenge to the autonomy of the professional worker, although the support for non-intervention could also be seen as protective.

Assessment of need

A parallel, but separate development to the case review system was undertaken by Westheimer (1977). Her analysis, that in the absence of formal prioritising systems workers will operate according to hidden, personal priorities, has implications for who receives a service, and the nature of the service offered. The latter being influenced by, for example, favoured methods of intervention of the worker or interest in particular client groups. Such an hypothesis has far reaching implications for service management in that it further argues that worker choice in workload allocation can improve efficiency and effectiveness by reducing irrational choices. Her further assertion, that 'when social workers are allocated too large a volume of work, they will define problems as less than they are' (1977, p79) suggests that service quality is put at risk in such situations.

Westheimer's (1977) conclusions, that caseload management involves close involvement of a supervisor over time, has similar drawbacks to those identified in Vickery's (1977) system; it can be labour intensive. Also, the assertion that it is not a mechanical exercise, but requires that both supervisor and social worker apply their diagnostic skills to categorising clients (Westheimer, 1977), reflects that this is a *case*load management system and not *work*load measurement or management. The whole scheme is predicated on assumptions that there will be close and regular supervision by an appropriately qualified person who can devote themselves to the exercise, and that the workloads of both allow time for such supervision.

Hence Lloyd-Owen's (1977) scheme, which elaborates the Westheimer position, allocates points on the basis of contact needs of the cases and then relates this to an arbitrary ceiling. The central premise is that 'objectives can be achieved only when the appropriate resource is available like social work skill, material resource and adequate time' (1977, p82). Hence categories are created which relate to the frequency of client contact required to achieve objectives identified as the result of diagnosis. So, for example, the stated objective of changing a clients behaviour would classify it as a Category A case, which would require weekly contact. In contrast, the objective of changing the material environment (e.g. change of accommodation or school) would be classified as Category F, and contact would be 'as required'. It is acknowledged that clients will move between categories, but essentially the management component is to categorise the cases according to the assessed needs, which are based on the nature of the social work intervention and are ultimately related to client contact.

The next stage of this process is to examine whether the caseload can be managed in the context of the other tasks in the workload and it is recommended that an eight week plan is drawn up, plotting all activities and planned contacts with those on the caseload, according to their category. This activity frequently reveals that there is not enough time to do all the work allocated, therefore the task is then to re-define the objectives, rather than assume that these can be achieved with less frequent client contact (Lloyd-Owen, 1977). This destroys the central plank of the scheme. If the aim of caseload management is to ensure a quality of service based on client need, it seems counter productive to re-define that need if there are not enough resources to meet it. This however is a crucial factor in the relationship between the task of measuring work and managing work. Are workload measurement schemes merely measuring work done, or do they ultimately require that ceilings are created and tasks prioritised? These questions need to be posed for any system, but the significant point about the Lloyd-Owen scheme is that it is accepted that time pressures should influence the outcomes. While she does suggest that, where objectives cannot be re-defined, this scheme can be used as evidence for increased staffing needs, but this is a moot point. If it is possible to re-define some objectives, why not all? In a climate of limited resources and arguments for efficiency, to suggest that the outcomes of intervention should be secondary to the resource allocation is a hostage to fortune.

Frequency of contact

Most critiques of workload measurement schemes start from the assumption that the number of cases a worker carries tells little about the amount of work that is undertaken, and there have been various attempts to quantify this. Above, the analysis was made on the frequency of contact determined by the assessed needs of the case. Another system which depends upon the number of planned contacts with a particular case, also incorporates notional timings (Osmond, Missing et al, 1977). In this system a pilot survey indicated that social worker-client contact averaged forty five minutes a week. Cases were then grouped into classifications based on the number of contacts required. These were associated with the

19

anticipated demands from certain categories of cases. The classification ranged from level one cases which would require two interviews per week to level five, where cases such as reviews of those in residential care would require an interview every twelve weeks.

The classification was accompanied by an estimate of how much of the total working week was spent in client contact. This estimate (20% or 14 interviews) provided an arbitrary ceiling for caseloads which were then constructed by a mix of cases from each of the categories. Cases were assessed at allocation and categorised by the number of interviews per week that they require and allocated to the worker who had space in their weekly interviewing schedule.

Such a system has less management intervention in the handling of cases, but nevertheless requires some relationship between the assessment of the case and the frequency of contact. Generally this related to the type of case, e.g.child protection, residential care, rather than the nature of the social work intervention that was required. No prescription was being made about what should be achieved in the two interviews per week. It also acknowledges that social workers have tasks in the working week other than interviewing clients, although no precise allocation of time is given to this. In fact 80% of social worker time is not managed at all in this scheme. In making the calculation about time spent with clients, the scheme also introduced the concept of a workload ceiling, although gave no indication of what should be done if the ceiling is reached, or if no worker has space on their caseload.

Priority based rationing systems

The response to the criticism that workload or caseload measurement schemes did not necessary lead to rationing or prioritising work had been addressed in some detail by Algie (1971). With Miller (1976) he devised an Operational Priority Systems (OPS) which was not just about time saving and management, but reflected broad policies about controlling the flow of work into an organisation. Using a variety of matrices priorities are assessed at the level of the organisation, not worker-level or even individual client-level. At the centre of the allocation system is client-problem dictionary with seven categories of functioning. These are used to predetermine assessment of both timing and nature of the intervention. Work is then allocated, starting with the most 'severe' cases, or at least those identified as having highest priority. Once all the available time has been allocated the 'lowest level non-priority groups' are not assigned to a worker. Within this scheme there is scope for variation of, for example, the notional times agreed. It is a way of rationing and offers guidance to teams on assessing, allocating and reviewing the work of the team and how to close the gap between planners' priority decisions and field workers' practice priorities.

Parsloe (1981) demonstrates that many other schemes have accepted the basis of the Algie and Miller model of operational priority, although different definitions of need have been utilised, or different units of measure allocated. However, she concludes that the more detailed systems are complicated to apply and time consuming. As such they are of limited value to team leaders of small teams, who are more likely to use informed, off-the-cuff decision making processes. A further limitation is that the categorisation is of the cases, and not of other work in which social workers are involved. How does a team or an agency decide on the relative priorities of, for example, offering an emergency duty system or visiting cases already referred and allocated?

In giving an overview of a number of systems, Parsloe (1981) concludes that all relied ultimately on the professional judgements of workers. This might suggest that, if they cannot adequately capture work done, or cannot be used effectively to control demand, then the processes of measuring and managing workloads are superfluous. However, she also determined that 'social workers have little doubt that being involved in a workload management system is in itself a useful exercise, which sharpens their perceptions and helps them to think more clearly about their work. Whether using the instruments is as advantageous as designing them has yet to be seen' (Parsloe, 1981 p87).

Significantly, Parsloe makes specific reference to workload management systems, thus reflecting a basic point that to measure workload is in itself not enough. The process of devising the schemes draws attention to the demands and constraints on workers, and to the complexities of the work in which they are involved. This information is fundamental to good management and, as the next example will show, schemes which can replicate this on a regular basis often do ensure that they are used consistently and effectively.

Workload management schemes

In echoing Parsloe's reservations about simple measurement systems, Bradley (Glastonbury et al, 1987) describes the translation of the case review system (CRS) and OPS into a workload management system, where the process of agreeing the system was as important as the outcome. The scheme devised attempts to reflect an objective measurement of work, with a capacity to reflect workload pressure. In social services departments, intervention can sometimes involve contact with more than one person in the family, different levels of responsibility or intervention and this has to be reflected in a workload management scheme. Because of differential work within cases 'a straightforward enumeration of cases carried by each team member was almost meaningless' (Glastonbury et al, 1987, p75). Moreover, the system devised attempts to address criticisms of other schemes, that they did not include the range of social work tasks. A measurement scale which could also be applied to other work, for example student supervision and groupwork, was agreed.

The result was a point score which was an amalgam of level of activity, partly drawn from a time per task analysis, and increments for responsibility. For example, a complex family situation where the worker carries more than one member or section of the family, and where crisis is perpetual, requiring action several times per week over the month would score four. If the worker was also prime worker with a child registered on the Non-Accidental Injury register (now called Child Protection register) an additional two points would be allocated. Student supervision carried five points per month.

Parsloe (1981) criticised workload measurement schemes because they can reward workers whose cases do not apparently improve, who continue to be involved over time. Work involved in the continuation of cases is less demanding that taking on new ones. The Bradley scheme answered this criticism by allocating extra points for new cases, or for taking on work in a new area which involved working with new legislation. The scheme also had notional workloads, or ceilings, differentially allocated according to individual workers role and position in the workforce. A qualified and experienced social worker would have a ceiling of forty five points per month, an experienced, but an unqualified worker would have a ceiling of thirty five points per calendar month. Although these ceilings were somewhat arbitrary there was the opportunity for a 'dynamic approach to caseload management' (1987, p76), which involved staff flexibility to take on more work in times of bombardment. Cynics might argue that such flexibility challenges the whole purpose of a workload management scheme. More positively, the ceilings gave justification for refusing pieces of work, thus achieving a more open and defensible rationing system. It was this staff involvement and the opportunity for review, both at a personal level and at regular intervals in the team settings, which was the strength of the scheme. The scheme also depended upon, or indeed created, an open system of management in an attempt at equitable distribution of work.

The criticism of such a scheme, and many like it, is that devising the points allocation and ceiling seems arbitrary, and it is here that the system may be open to abuse, with staff exaggerating contact. Also, the system is always retrospective, telling workers and their managers how busy they were, and only being partially successful in anticipating workloads. However the system of management, which is inherent in the review of workloads in supervision sessions, does allow for 'fallow' periods to compensate a worker after a period of stress. The weakness of the system, and perhaps of all systems in social work, is that when the work flow increased and all workers were working to their ceilings there was an informal 'audit' which might prioritise case closure and produce space, but at the end of it all workers merely went above their ceilings and, where this happened regularly, the ceiling was raised.

Time per task systems

Many of the systems outlined above depend in some way on a measurement of time, whether this is in number of interviews, frequency of contact or units which reflect the amount of time spent with particular cases. Time is incorporated into a different accounting system, or unit of measurement, often by the inclusion of another level of assessment. The latter, which are designed to reflect need or intervention levels, have been criticised as being imprecise and open to abuse because of the variables that may be operating in the assessment. A system which has attempted to be as objective as possible, is one which relies solely on the notion of the time taken to perform task, based on initial measurements which can feed into the allocation of a time for a particular task. The most well defined workload measurement system on this basis is that operated by the probation service, where each unit of work is linked to a time measurement and workloads are measured against nationally agreed timings for a working week/month. Davies, Dyson, Lynch and Miller (1988) describe a similar system implemented in a local authority social services department, but the probation service scheme was first introduced in 1972 and has been refined over time in an attempt to achieve a level of accuracy. It is the critique of this work which led to the research described in the following chapters.

The initial probation scheme was devised by the National Association of Probation Officers (NAPO) in partnership with the then Conference of Chief Probation Officers. The workloads identified were based on the statutory duties of the probation service and timings were allocated on this basis. Hence the scheme calculated, or more accurately made an informed guess about, how long in each month an individual probation officer spent supervising an individual offender who was subject to a probation order. This calculation therefore made assumptions about how frequently contact was made, and how long each contact lasted. These calculations very soon became outdated because criminal justice legislation in 1972 and 1973 changed the nature of some of the tasks, and increased the number of statutory duties of the service.

Recognising this, and the fact that the timings were to a large extent arbitrary, in 1977 the Home Office undertook the National Activity Recording Survey (NARS), which involved the largest survey of demands made upon the services of the probation officers. The methodology involved probation officers recording their activity every fifteen minutes. This data was then aggregated to devise a time per task weighting for the various duties of the probation service. For example, the time officers spent supervising individuals on probation was collected during a specified period. An average weighting for the supervision of a probation order was calculated as 120 minutes (two hours) per month. The overall results were then the subject of negotiation and the revised version, Probation Service Workload Measurement (PSWM) was published in 1979 (Appendix 1). A further part of the equation for the probation service management of workloads is that the allocation of a time per task facilitated the measurement of work allocated against the negotiated hours in the codes and conditions of service. Ultimately an average workload was expected to equate to the 150 hours per four week period which was negotiated in the 1984 Codes and Conditions of Service.

A strength of the PSWM over other schemes was that it allowed for the inclusion of work other than that directly related to clients. To ensure that a direct equation could be made on a monthly basis an allocation was included for annual leave, sick leave and attending courses. This allowance included the possibility for local variations. There was also included a 'personal special allowance' which included 'kindred social work, the giving of lectures, attendance at meetings and general "back-up"' (see Appendix 1). Office duty and court duty were calculated separately and given a weighting, as was student supervision.

While this scheme was worked out precisely, building on a national study of the workloads of probation officers, it is still open to criticism. Coulshed (1990) has commented that such systems are mechanistic, and professionals are not clock watchers. This may be true, but the basis of the scheme enabled the probation service over a decade to be able to calculate resource needs on the basis of such a formula, and this has meant that, until recent years, it has been protected from the cash limiting that other public services have experienced. More pertinent to this discussion is that the weightings have also enabled NAPO to conduct discussions and negotiations about workload ceilings, and have focused attention on prioritising work. Hence the scheme has been able to meet the requirements of management in relation to resource calculations, and of front line workers by providing some protection.

However the scheme has been subject to more detailed criticism of the basis of the calculations which arose out of the application of the formula to the workloads of a probation team (Glastonbury et al, 1987). It was this analysis which led to the recognition that further research was needed some of which is the basis of this text. The most compelling criticism of this scheme can also be made of many workload schemes, that is it describes work done, but makes no allowance, takes no account of the quality of that work. At the inception of the scheme NAPO argued that it 'explores the possibility of establishing from our results ways of assessing the volume of work which can be undertaken consistent with best professional practice' (NAPO, 1972, p5). However throughout the development of the scheme there has been little emphasis on ensuring that the work measured was undertaken to any standard, or incorporated best professional practice. In this way the scheme moved away from those documented earlier in this chapter, which involved close involvement of the worker and their supervisor in the assessment of the needs of individual cases. Official descriptions have always acknowledged that the PSWM was a measure of the quantity of the work undertaken, and not the quality.

One further set of issues arising out of the NARS exercise need to be discussed before moving on to a more substantive description of the research based on this model. Many of the weightings derived from NARS were challenged before the revised workloads were published in 1979, the most contentious of which was that allocated to the preparation of social inquiry reports. The purpose and process of preparing a social inquiry report is described in the next chapter, but suffice it to say at this point that they were documents prepared for the courts by probation officers in a given time scale (usually three weeks) and involved an assessment of the individual, the offence and the likely response to the involvement of the probation service. The 1972 weightings had identified four hours as the average time for preparing such a report, but the NARS study recorded a figure of 135 minutes for the preparation of these reports, and suggested a weighting of three hours. This was disputed by NAPO and a compromise of three and a half hours (210 minutes) was offered. This compromise was not acceptable to NAPO who argued in a letter to chief probation officers that 'good professional practice' required the retention of the original weightings. This argument was not successful, and the weighting of 210 minutes stood until a further revision of the workloads was undertaken in 1990. This dispute is significant because it reflects three strands which are the basis of the research described in the following chapters. The first is that the preparation of reports is a significant and discrete task for the probation service, and as such provides a useful focus for workload research. Second, NAPO have been consistent in their argument that, while workload measurement was to protect workers' code and conditions of service, it also had an important function in protecting the quality of service offered to offenders. Summarising the position, the then General Secretary of NAPO, wrote 'members will also be concerned to maintain services to clients but do them no service by agreeing to work when tired and strained by long working hours. Clients are best served by a well-resourced probation staff with enough staff' (Beaumont, NAPO, 1986). Here is the essence of workload weighting schemes, however they are devised. They can never accurately measure the extent of the work done, but they are necessary as part of effective management to ensure equitable distribution of work. Finally, the use of timings, and arguments about differences of thirty minutes, raise questiona about whether there can ever be hair trigger precision in the logging of social work activities.

25

Conclusion

In this chapter themes which have emerged from a review of attempts to devise effective workload systems are documented. This review includes an analysis of the measurements that have been used to capture the work of social workers and the way that such measurements have been incorporated into workload management systems.

The most stringent criticism, and the one most difficult to refute, is that they are open to abuse. This suggests that social workers will manipulate the work that they undertake to try and present themselves as more busy than they really are. Such criticism raises questions about the purpose of workload measurement and management systems. If, as has been argued in this chapter, they are there to provide protection for workers, as well as information for management about necessary resources, then there is no need for them to be abused. More relevantly, a major limitation of most of the systems, that they merely record work already done, rather than providing a mechanism for allocation of future work, suggests that there is little point in abusing the systems.

More pertinent is the criticism that no system can allow for variation in stamina and skill between workers and the risk of all is that they operate at the lowest common denominator. In doing this they can be criticised as being mechanistic and 'to this extent they are anti-professional and this may be the hidden cost which needs to be acknowledged' (Parsloe, 1981 p77). However, the benefits which are inherent in systems which are dynamic, or based on open management are obvious. Social workers not only have their pressures recognised and documented, but some schemes provide for management support in difficult decisions about allocating time. It is often these which put social workers most at risk. Decisions not to visit a family in which there is ultimately a child abuse inquiry, or not to take breach action against an offender who subsequently re-offends, are sometimes made because of demands on time. Workload systems which document overtly the need for priority rating, and the basis on which those priorities are decided, ultimately provide protection.

Throughout the chapter it has become evident that, although some schemes work on a principle of prioritising, few have clear mechanisms for deciding upon principles of rationing, or identifying workload ceilings. To do this requires management decisions, but also systems for accurately capturing all the work done. In reviewing a system which has attempted to capture comprehensively the work undertaken by the probation service, a further limitation has been identified. The methodology used to inform decisions about how long probation officers spend on particular tasks did not take into account the quality of the work undertaken, but merely logged work done. It is the attention to hair trigger precision of time, combined with lack of attention to quality of work done which stimulated the research described in the following chapters.

2 Defining the task

Introduction

Researching workloads in social work raises specific questions about the nature and extent of the social work task, or its component parts. There is no agreement about what constitutes the social work task, or more precisely, there are many strands to the task which can not readily be disentangled from each other. This chapter, in reflecting on the workload schemes outlined, will address some of the complexities of researching workloads in social work. In preparation for the description of a specific piece of research there will be a discussion of how a particular task was identified. The preparation of reports for court by the probation service holds a central place in the work of the service. As a discrete assessment event, report preparation has parallels in all social work agencies, voluntary and statutory. Discussion of policy guidelines and research on best practice in preparing court reports will provide background to the specific research project described in the following chapters.

Researching workloads

Throughout social work history there has been some form of counting in workloads. There has also been dissatisfaction with the methods of counting. This is because different pieces of work need different amounts of attention and therefore have different amounts of time spent on them;

different individuals demand different levels of attention, and different methods or styles of social work intervention take up differing amounts of time. Added to this, social workers spend time in a great many tasks which are not directly related to cases. Even when work is only indirectly related to cases e.g. travelling and case recording, it can still take up a significant amount of time but is not necessarily calculated as contributing to cases. Finally, social workers themselves have different capacities, strengths and weaknesses. These justifications for having some sophisticated form of workload measurement also constitute the reasons why devising such a measurement is so difficult, and why conducting research relating to the task of devising the measure is so fraught.

Further complexities in researching workloads are inherent in the role of the researcher, and the purpose for which the research is being undertaken. There is a continuing irony that research to improve working conditions has to worsen temporarily those conditions by adding to the tasks. This is illustrated by a diary exercise constructed to compile an audit of social work activity (Orme, 1989a). Workers participating took delight in logging accurately the time spent completing the diaries, even when other tasks were not so systematically reported. Additionally, researching workloads involves investigating the activity of social workers. In doing this, it appears to question their professional autonomy, challenging both what they do and why they do it. Historically, such oversight has been the remit of professional supervision sessions, often related to the needs of the client and not to discussions about the organisation of the working day.

However, in highlighting issues of measurement and management, both researchers and managers are demanding information about how social workers spend their time and on what they spend their time. Managers such as Bradley (Glastonbury et al, 1987) are also asking about the individual work with clients which relates to assessments based on particular methods of intervention, which then demand a particular point allocation. This constitutes a challenge to professional autonomy. However, this challenge is not necessarily a negative imposition. Social workers in many fields have acknowledged the need for some control of their workloads. The probation service has argued consistently that some managed allocation of work needs to be undertaken, and social workers in other organisations have identified lack of workload measurement and management as a source of stress (NALGO, 1989). Underlying such observations is the need for protection of individual workers, not only from the stress of having too much to do, but also from the consequences of not having time to undertake work to the highest quality, which includes giving appropriate time to individuals and families. If workers are to be given such protection there is a need for a more open accounting system of the work in which they are involved.

Researching workloads therefore is not merely a mechanistic counting of what is done, but is integrally linked to the effectiveness of social work intervention. Much has been written about the benefits of effectiveness research (Sheldon, 1988), and its contribution to the social work task, but in the current political climate there are two measures of effectiveness. These are meeting targets, where these are set by the agency or some other authority, and meeting the aims of the agency, where these aims are assumed to be congruent with the needs of the service users. Research in the area of workloads and effectiveness has to discern whether it is possible to monitor targets such as whether a certain number of clients have been seen, or tasks undertaken (eg report preparation) in a given time and to an appropriate standard. While matters of time can be monitored by internal mechanisms, the value of independent, or external, research is that it can contribute to the debate about the quality of service delivery and best practice without being identified with a managerial or political agenda. The danger for the researcher, however, is that, in a climate of managerialism, findings can be interpreted in a way which was unintended and can be used for other ends.

Implications for workers

For those engaged in the performance of the social work task to wait for long term surveys and results is as useful as having a workload measuring system that tells them that they were very busy last month. No matter how precise the measuring system, it is useless unless incorporated into some form of management system. Similarly, no matter how significant the research findings, if they cannot be applied to the everyday experience of the practitioners they are of limited value.

Everitt et al (1992) summarise some of the challenges to researching in area of workloads. In identifying an 'emerging paradigm' (1992, p123) they explore the inter-relationship between performance review, monitoring and quality assurance. Information is collected in social work agencies for a number of purposes, and this influences the response of workers to any research task, which is usually one of resistance. In the case of workload measurement research, resistance is greater because the focus of attention is on workers' performance, however defined, but often includes data which is collected for other purposes: monthly and annual statistics, travelling claim forms, claims for time off in lieu are just some examples. Everitt et al (1992) challenge the assumption that quality control and inspection units, as methods of evaluation, will automatically ensure improvements in practice, but suggest that 'this form of evaluation will submerge questions about what is good practice and will legitimate particular forms of practice based on positivist techniques and supposed objectivity and neutrality' (1992, p125). Such a note of caution also has to be applied to researching workload measurement, because of the increasing association of measurement with performance indicators.

That social workers often experience research as existing on a different plane, irrelevant to their real concerns (Raynor, 1984), is important when researching workloads, as is the criticism that researchers are seen to exploit practitioners for their own ends of publication and academic status.

Significantly, the acknowledgement of power bases within research has resonance for activities which can be identified with a managerial imperative, and this includes researching workloads. It might be assumed that when research commissioned by organisations such as trade union, would not be vulnerable to resistance and criticism. However, the difficulties are only marginally improved. Whoever commissions the research, certain methodologies require the researcher to remain detached. Also once the results are published there is no guarantee that they will not be exploited.

The problematic of evaluating practice is intensified when researching workloads. The identification of how long workers take to perform tasks inevitably raises questions about what tasks are performed and, for management purposes, is inexorably tied to why are the particular task is being undertaken.

To conduct research which simply measures how long it takes to perform tasks risks criticism that such work is reductionist, based on a crude empiricism which merely counts the units of measure which 'should' be allocated to the task. Such criticisms beg the definition of empiricism. Even measuring how long a task takes raises questions such as: can the task be defined? can the process be measured and what units of measure are appropriate?

Social work tasks which are timed, monitored or measured can be described by various indicators. In the case of reports written for courts, for example, official circulars provide one set of indicators for what have been described as negotiations with courts (Raynor, 1980), but another set is provided by social work discourse on, for example, diagnosis (Curnock & Hardiker, 1979; Sainsbury, 1970); crisis intervention (O'Hagan, 1986), short term intervention (Reid & Epstein, 1972). In acknowledging the complexity of definitions of social work tasks Raynor has warned that 'without an awareness of the(se) normative and interpretative dimensions of the social worker's task and the conceptual equipment to consider them rationally (if not scientifically) the empiricist approach to technical effectiveness is insufficient guide' (Raynor, 1984, p9). Naive reductionism in the area of workload measurement denies the complexities of the task, ignores issues of effectiveness and accountability, and lends itself to 'unwitting ideological bias through its failure to consider political and moral issues' (Raynor, 1984, p9). As will be seen in the final chapter of this text, ideological bias, political and moral issues are central to issues of workload measurement, and to deny them puts the very profession of social work at risk.

30

As described in Chapter 1, research in the area of workload measurement in the probation service has been based on the National Activity Recording Study (NARS). This study was designed to provide accurate systematic and detailed information about the time devoted to various tasks. While not a time and motion study, it was apparent to observers that officers were anxious to be seen to be using their time well and performing tasks more quickly (Glastonbury et al, 1987). There was no attempt or intention to link activity levels to effectiveness or to best professional practice although it was conceded that 'allocation of time does not of itself give any measure of effectiveness but consideration of actual as distinct from the expected use of time may be helpful improving effectiveness' (NARS, 1979).

After consultation, the NARS figures were used to update the Probation Service Workload Measurement (PSWM) figures which had been established in 1972. When this revision occurred in 1979, it was acknowledged that a review would be needed in the mid-1980s mainly because of the increasing tasks the probation service was taking on which did not have a measure. Community service, for example, was in existence when the scales were devised but was not given an allocation of time per task. In any of the systems outlined in the previous chapter the research task is to the analyze and evaluate the appropriateness or accuracy of the measurements. The initial difficulty for research into this area is to avoid getting into an escalating spiral of using research data to increase the accuracy of measurements to hair trigger precision. It is not possible in a profession which is constantly dealing with the unpredictability of human beings, both the clients and the workers, to establish a predictive measure which will cover all eventualities. What research can offer is the opportunity to consider a number of variables in the tasks undertaken which need to be included in any measurement system. Ironically, but not surprisingly, the very nature of the material being researched creates problems and issues for the design and process of the research which reflect some of the issues for the process of workload measurement itself.

The limitations of projects to date is that primarily they have been concerned with activity and measurement, but it does not have to be so. The workload management scheme in a social services department described by Bradley (Glastonbury et al, 1987), although not the subject of independent research, was originally based on an experimental exercise itself derived from Prime's work (1977). It had built into it opportunity for reviews and revisions which were deliberately made part of the management process of the measurement exercise, acknowledging the arbitrary nature of the original ceiling levels. The initial review held some twenty two months after the implementation of the scheme raised some

31

important issues about weightings allocated. Some of these were to do with creating categories for weighting which had not previously been included, and others were about amending weightings which had been allocated. Once amendments were made, the system operated on the basis of individual supervision which included assessment of cases for the purposes of allocating a weighting and assessing the total workload of the individual worker, measuring this against the agreed ceiling.

Observations made on the basis of the review have implications for researching workloads. In the first instance, the arbitrary nature of the weightings and ceilings is acknowledged. Also, the system might be open to abuse by workers over reporting the extent or nature of the contact, and the nature of the measurements might reward cases which do not improve. Such issues are pertinent to a research task focusing on measurement of workloads.

The benefits of having work pressure identified in some measurable form for workers outweighs some of the disadvantages and can be used to engage staff in the research process. However the significance of who undertakes the research, where the funding is coming from and the possible uses of the results of the research are obvious concerns for those who might be the 'subjects' or 'objects' of such research. Hence the criticism of the weightings which emerged out of the exercise undertaken by the Home Office in 1978 for probation officers which involved the allocation of a time per task measure for most activities of the probation service were that they did not accord with workers' perception of how long tasks took to perform. The benefits of the analysis were that the resulting Probation Service Workload Measure (PSWM) included notional timings for tasks other than cases, and allowed for locally agreed weightings for tasks which related to particular circumstances. By including personal weightings for holidays, sickness in monthly 'scores', and making an equation between miles travelled and time weightings, this measure aimed at a high level of precision in calculating workloads which, as previously stated, was to equate with an agreed working month.

These benefits were not acknowledged in the ensuing negotiations which focused on two limitations of the study. The first was that the method of collecting data for the initial weightings was open to criticism. Workers logging their activities on a 15 minute interval were anxious to show how busy they are. No matter how much they are reassured, the 'time and motion' factor will come into play. Davies et al (1973) observe that workload measurement is a potentially threatening form of analysis which can lead to an overstatement of work being done. This may be particularly relevant when the organisation monitoring the activity is the Government Department to whom the worker is ultimately accountable and not an independent research body. The themes of pay, piper and tune are explored by Everitt et al (1992, p129), and while it is possible to applaud the sentiments that being research minded should mean being autonomous, it is more difficult to be perceived as such when researching the very essence of the pay, and the tune.

In the NARS study it is suggested that officers were not overstating what they did, they merely did more because of the nature of the data collection. To use a calculation of time spent on individual tasks during the period of monitoring as a basis for calculating 'ideal' workloads is therefore based on a false analysis, and no emphasis is given for performing tasks to 'best professional practice'.

The second limitation of the NARS exercise was that timings equated to tasks, irrespective of factors which might impinge upon these tasks. Hence all social inquiry reports were calculated as taking three hours, irrespective of a number of possible variables. There is an argument that these variables would even out over a number of reports, but no account was taken of possible differentials, so that they could be considered when allocating workloads. While the monitoring of activities in the NARS was a perfectly acceptable method of collecting data related to workloads, it is only when it is linked with such fine calculations, and when these are linked to resource allocation, that it becomes the subject of scrutiny and challenge.

Social workers are extremely undisciplined at recording their activities. A point which has been echoed in the second report of the Financial Management Information Systems Project Team to the Probation Service (Home Office, 1989b). The task of recalling and recording is an onerous one when looking at workloads. Ironically, as has been said at the beginning of this chapter, it adds to the workload and becomes a pressure. In the diary exercise described earlier (Orme, 1989a) staff were anxious to show **how** busy they were, but not very consistent at recording what they were busy doing. For example, in a part of the survey auditing work in prisons, one probation officer logged that she spent three hours recording on her caseload on a Sunday, but did not note which cases were being recorded - the information could not therefore be attributed to individual cases, and was redundant for the purposes of the survey. The need for constant chivvying and reminding of the focus of the task in such a research project is apparent.

Constraints under which social workers are operating at any one time will also affect recorded measurements and may negate attempts to get a 'best possible practice' measure built in, and therefore influence the research conclusions. A team whose work was being recorded in another survey were supposed to be operating a workload ceiling which should allow space to achieve best possible practice. The particular month which was monitored coincided with a high level of activity in the courts, but there was no policy of rationing or prioritising. In accepting all reports allocated, officers were under instructions from their manager to do only one social inquiry report interview in order to be able to respond to the demand. This instruction was contrary to best practice as laid down in

Home Office guidelines. Not all officers complied with the instruction, but this meant challenging a management decision and illustrates the tension that workers experience between co-operating with a research project and complying with a management instruction. In any research project involving social workers 'in situ' it is not possible to create the best possible environment i.e. reducing the number of variables.

Having identified negative factors and limitations in researching workloads it is important to acknowledge the benefits for the workers involved. The involvement of any worker in a research project gives a sense of importance, self worth and an recognition that what they are doing is in some way significant. In studies to date there has also been a rather perverse sense of relief at having excess workloads acknowledged by some system of measurement was present in the probation service. In 1985 an exercise was undertaken to administer the NARS workload weightings to the workloads of one probation office for one month. The purpose of this was twofold, to evaluate the weightings which were currently allocated to tasks and to evaluate the relevance of having a workload measurement system (Glastonbury et al, 1987). This analysis was retrospective. Statistical returns and mileage claims for one month were analyzed against the against weightings, where they existed. This analysis was then presented to the teams, and their observations were noted. In terms of the research task, the pressure from the officers was to devise a measure that was even more precise than the one in existence. They confirmed that it was comforting to have evidence that they **were** overworked but they wanted it acknowledged just how much they were overworked. The relevance of this demand seemed limited because the information was telling how overworked they **had been** and gave no predictive statement about future levels of overwork. This latter exercise would demand a different order of information and would depend upon how far the measures accurately reflected the task. However, even precise measurements, or continuous time recording systems will have difficulty predicting the likely demand from, for example, courts or offenders. The potential for workload measurement schemes to resolve dilemmas or reduce stress is limited, this requires workload management. Hence Bradley's scheme (Glastonbury et al, 1987) was part of an ongoing individual case review system, but even this did not resolve the problems because when there were increased work demands, the ceilings were raised. A workload management scheme, in its most positive sense, involves setting ceilings and when these are reached, devising rationing and prioritising mechanisms. Such systems not only protect workers, they help to ensure the quality of the service. The notion of workload management is, however, also highly contested in social work, and will be discussed in more detail in chapter six.

Researching the social work task

Before moving on to describe in detail the particular research project devised to attempt to meet some of the criticisms of workload measurement, it is necessary to return to a specific problem of researching workloads in social work. This relates to the complexity of the definition of what is social work and what constitutes a social work task. To enable work to be measured there is a need to deconstruct the social work task into some component parts. The challenge is to undertake this deconstruction in a way that is relevant to the activities of social workers, and in a way that is measurable. Intervention by social workers can be categorised in many different ways. For example, client groups can be identified within caseloads and a generic social worker could be working with older persons, children and people with disabilities; a probation officer could be working with probationers or ex-prisoners. However, within these groups social workers might be using similar forms of social work intervention which might include crisis intervention, task centred casework or behaviour modification. Alternatively, the worker might be involved in one to one work, group work or community work. A further method of analyzing social workers' tasks is by the stage of the work, that is the point in the process. These are usually categorised as reception, assessment, on-going work and endings. All of these definitions or categories can be subsumed under headings which relate to the remit for the worker to be involved. So, for example, an assessment can be undertaken for the purposes of allocating resources under the Children Act (1989), identifying need under the National Health Service and Community Care Act (1990) or the preparation of a court report under the Criminal Justice Act (1991).

The workload measurement schemes identified in the previous chapter highlight that a number of categories can be used to analyze workloads. Type of case, type of intervention or specific task, related to, for example, court order, are some of the categories used to date. However, if workload schemes are to be challenged, or even if they are to be refined, by the research process it is necessary to identify a particular category, or way of defining an activity, which is transferrable across social work activities. Also, it is important to identify a piece of work which can be perceived as discrete, not part of ongoing work which can be calculated differently, or can be included in another task. For example the notion of double counting was of concern in the analysis of duty work in the critique of NARS (Glastonbury et al, 1987). Probation officers were expected to be available to see clients, but while on duty they could be using the time to perform administrative tasks, or supervise others on the caseloads, which would also be counted. Similarly the disadvantages of joint work not being acknowledged is highlighted by groupwork, which might involve two probation officers running the group, under a supervision order held by a third. The allocation of a probation order would allow for a once only recording on the caseload of the supervising officer. The total work would be subsumed under the average weighting for probation supervision.

The task of writing a court report constitutes a discrete activity in the workload of a probation officer which is readily accessible to measurement. As an assessment event it has parallels in other social work agencies, voluntary and statutory.

Social inquiry reports

Writing reports for court has been integral to the work of the probation service since its inception at the beginning of this century. Reports for the criminal courts have been called alternatively social enquiry reports, social inquiry reports and now pre-sentence reports. At the time that the research described in this text was undertaken probation officers were writing social inquiry reports(SIRs), and it is this term that will be used from now on. The function of report writing is to enable a probation officer to present a social history to the courts, to present the offender in context and to contribute to an explanation for his or her offending behaviour. A report also includes an opinion (framed as a recommendation or proposal) on how effective intervention by the probation service might be in the overall behaviour and social context of the offender. This twofold function means that report writing constitutes a central activity within the workload of the probation service, acting as a filter for the total workload, targeting the work of the service and providing a blueprint or workplan for what will follow.

On the one hand, it is argued that social inquiry reports are 'only descriptions of circumstances in accordance with official definitions of their purpose' (Curnock & Hardiker, 1979 p12; Davies, 1974) On the other, they parallel other assessment processes in the social and health care fields if it is accepted that 'an assessment is a perceptual/analytic process of selecting, categorising, organising and synthesising data: it is both a process and a product of our understanding' (Coulshed, 1989, p13). Court reports draw upon the professional skills and knowledge of the worker to communicate with individuals and families, collecting and collating information and reflecting upon this in the light of existing theoretical and research knowledge. This is supplemented by information from other sources, including the opinions of other professionals and relevant individuals.

The process of writing a court report therefore parallels the preparation of social histories in medical settings, investigations in child at risk cases and assessments for the purpose of allocation of resources under care management. In each of these instances Curnock and Hardiker's claim for social enquiry reports is relevant, 'whatever the setting, the social work

36

relationship has a specific context, boundary and purpose' (1979, p15). Specific guidelines for writing reports by probation officers are considered in detail below but the direct correlation of the task of writing court reports to general social work activity, as opposed to probation specific activity, is acknowledged in the DHSS booklet *Reports to Courts: Practice Guidance for Social Workers* (1987).

The usefulness of focusing on the task of report writing in the context of researching workload measurement is evident. It provides a discrete intervention which is universally applicable. Additionally, the need for report writing to be to be performed to the highest level of professional expertise is also apparent. The outcome of any assessment event, or process, has implications for an agency in that it influences the workload either by offering a service, or diverting the potential user of the service. The implication for those being assessed is even more crucial, in that the outcome may be further intervention by social work agencies, with all the attendant consequences. The decision by the assessing agency not to intervene further can also have impact in that service will not be made available, which may influence the quality of life of the individual. In the case of reports for criminal courts, such decisions can lead to a loss of liberty.

For the purposes of the researching workloads in the probation service, the social inquiry report is a useful vehicle for studying the correlation between workload measurement and management. In particular, it offers the opportunity to challenge the principles on which work in this area to date has been based. It also offers the opportunity to research a discrete task within social work and to offer some assessment of the performance of this task, both in terms of the time taken to complete the task and the standard to which the task was performed. Finally, as a task which results in a document prepared for another audience, it is possible to acquire feedback on and evaluation of the performance of the task, therefore enabling a correlation between efficiency and effectiveness to be made. Moreover, there is a substantive body of writing and research which documents the expectations of the process and outcome of preparing social enquiry reports.

In documenting the trends in court report writing during the 1980s, Bottoms and Stelman (1988) plot how shifts in criminal justice policy, as reflected in the passing of the Criminal Justice Act 1982 for example, helped to concentrate the attention of local probation services on the task to be performed, namely what kind of report writing should be developed to meet the requirements of the Act. This was followed in 1984 by a direct statement by the Home Office which offered guidance to probation officers on a number of practice issues. The Statement of National Objectives and Priorities for the Probation Service in England and Wales (Home Office, 1984) gave no guidance on the content of reports, only the targeting. Content issues were addressed in Home Office Circulars, and in 1983 two separate circulars recommended greater specificity in the task of writing reports, including guidance for including sources of information and that recommendations be supported with reasons. This was followed by a much more extensive statement (Home Office Circular 92/1986) which dealt with the circumstances in which reports should be prepared, for the first time suggesting report writers address cultural factors and offending histories.

In tracing the history of report writing in the probation service Bottoms and Stelman (1988) identify three historical approaches to the preparation of reports, which include 'scientism', research and theorisation (p28); penal welfare strategies which echo the 'hierarchical observations and normalising judgements' described by Foucault (1977, p184) and Giller's 'blueprint for action' (Morris and Giller, 1987, p218). Their development of these themes into recommendations for writing reports tries to provide ways in which practice can most closely follow and express professional social work knowledge, skills and values, while at the same time remaining consistent with the demand placed upon the report writer by legislation and official guidance. This is consistent with their emphatic view that social inquiry reports are social work documents (Bottoms & Stelman, 1988, chpt 2). It is this combination of factors which makes the preparation of social inquiry reports (SIRs) a useful focus for researching issues of workload management in social work.

More significantly, Bottoms and Stelman's claim that their aim in writing guidance on SIRs was to help ensure 'best professional practice' (1988, p120) has resonance with the aims of the research project described in the following chapters. The critiques of workload measurement schemes in the preceding chapter, that they measure how much is done, and how long it takes, but that they do not measure the quality of the work undertaken need to be met. It is apparent that focusing a particular task will eliminate variables. That there is guidance on how to perform that task to achieve quality practice gives some yardstick against which quality and professional practice can be measured.

It is the pivotal position of writing court reports in the probation service that has meant that, throughout the history of workload measurement schemes, the time allocation given to the task has been hotly disputed (NAPO, 1972; NARS, 1978). A negative definition of reports as 'often hasty judgements made under considerable pressure, on the basis of inadequate information' (Walker and Beaumont, 1981, p16), is counteracted by Bottoms and Stelman's attempts to give guidance on writing high quality reports. However they identify three practice issues which influence the preparation of SIRs: time, routinization, and use of language (1988, p14). Commenting on feedback from practitioners they acknowledge that 'it was common to hear people say that the report was not as good as they would have liked because of the shortness of the time to prepare it, and the pressure of other work time' (1988, p16). This corroborates McWilliam's findings that 'in almost all instances where beliefs were compromised the shortage of time was either seen as being crucial in effect, or was cited as being so by the officers concerned' (1986, p459). Hence the direct link of the preparation of high quality reports with appropriate amounts of time to prepare them is well documented. Time, however, is not an independent variable, but one that is constrained by other factors, such as the demands and expectations of the court, as well as the demands of other pieces of work.

Conclusion

This chapter has commenced the process of outlining the background to the specific research project. An exploration of the difficulties involved researching social work practice led to a more specific outlining of the difficulties and benefits of researching workload measurement. At the heart of much of the debate is the difficulty of identifying the social work task, or more particularly isolating an aspect of the social work task which renders it possible to establish a relevant workload measure. Reports for court prepared by probation officers have been identified as a relevant piece of practice for the focus of this research. They have been chosen because they represent the universal social work task of assessment, it is possible to isolate a discrete process related to the preparation of reports and there is research and policy guidelines to help identify good practice. The centrality of report writing in the probation service, and the demands that they make of the officers preparing them has probably contributed to the attention that has been given to them in debates about workload schemes in the probation service. The fact that they have been at the centre of debate about the accuracy of existing workload measurement schemes is yet another reason for focusing on researching the preparation of social enquiry reports in workload research.

3 Probation service workloads

Introduction

Having identified some of criticisms of previous systems for measuring workloads this chapter seeks to explore further the strengths or limitations of the Probation Service Workloads Measurement System (PSWM). It takes as its starting point the limitations of the methodology which was used to arrive at the workload weightings. For reasons clarified in the previous chapter it focuses on the weightings allocated to the preparation of reports prepared for probation officers for the criminal courts. The aim of the specific research project was to test out the weighting using a different methodology, one which would allow probation officers, where possible, to prepare reports according to their understanding of best professional practice. Some calculation of the time this took would be undertaken, and comparisons made with the previous weightings.

To meet the criticisms of earlier work on workload weightings the research included an assessment of the quality of the reports by the authors of the report and by those on whom the reports were prepared. Additionally, criteria from research and policy documents which have been outlined in the previous chapter were used to test the effectiveness of the task and whether it constituted best practice according to an independent evaluation.

In undertaking this exercise it was also anticipated that component parts of preparing a court report would be captured and that issues related to the complexity of measuring workloads would inform conclusions about whether it is possible to measure social work workloads with any degree of accuracy, or more significantly, whether it is desirable.

Background

At the 1987 annual general meeting of NAPO there was evident dissatisfaction with the system of workload weightings which was then operating in the probation service. Two motions were tabled which drew direct attention to the limitations of the system. The motion which was passed nem con was worded as follows:

> The current system of workload measurement in the probation service is out of date and inadequate, and grossly underestimates the time needed for each task. This AGM therefore instructs the Probation Practice Committee to negotiate an urgent revision of all these measurements.

This both questioned the timings which had been allocated for tasks, and acknowledged that the weightings agreed in the PSWM in 1979 (Appendix 1) pre-dated criminal justice legislation which prescribed some of the tasks being undertaken by the probation service at that time. On this basis, the weightings had become out of date soon after they had been negotiated. It was argued that the system did allow for the accommodation of new legislative tasks, and that some policy and practice changes within the service did not lend themselves easily to a time per task weighting based on statutory duties. Such changes included groupwork and joint activities in the area of community service and day centre work. Additionally, the service provided for the courts, including involvement in bail schemes, and the work of the probation officers in prisons and hostels illustrated that the role of a probation officer was becoming much more diverse than the earlier analysis suggested. None of these were recognised in the PSWM.

A further issue raised by the methodology which produced the previous weightings was that they focused on the work of individual probation officers, not the input of work into cases. In diary exercises, or exercises which capture a snapshot of work at anyone time, it is the general pattern of work of an individual officer which is recorded. This leads to many imprecisions within the system, either because work is not captured or because it is counted twice. Specific attention was drawn to the problems caused by the weightings given to throughcare of those in institutions (Glastonbury et al, 1987). The time spent in travel to institutions could only be claimed by the officer claiming the mileage, and accompanying officer could not claim this time, which in some cases could be considerable. This meant that the overall calculation for throughcare would not reflect **all** officer time. Alternatively, it could be argued that

41

when an officer was undertaking office duty they would also be available to undertake administrative work, and see clients who were on supervision to them. This constituted double counting.

Other criticisms of the precision of the PSWM included questioning the allocation for aftercare supervision. Time spent on voluntary cases need not differ so much from that spent on licensees. The point at which an individual comes out of the institution might affect the input made by a supervising officer, irrespective of whether the after care is statutory or voluntary. Individual circumstances e.g. whether they are homeless or not, or whether they are simply a dependent or demanding person may also influence the input, again irrespective of the existence of any licence.

To a greater or lesser extent such variables are able to be calculated, and this merely involves changing the way in which the measurement is taken. For example, to accommodate the differential contact at different points of the order or supervision there could be a sliding scale which would reflect the minimum standards (or perhaps more positively, best practice) guidelines adopted by many services now. Another way to approach both this, and demands made by different individuals, is to change **what** is measured. The PSWM measures activity based on the statutory tasks of the Probation Service - report writing and the various forms of supervision. It might be possible to adopt a system of time weightings which would relate to the nature of the case e.g. type of offence, type of offender, type of intervention. Or, as some schemes have done, abandon the concept of allocating time weightings and allocate a point score for these or other variables, and fix an arbitrary ceiling. As was demonstrated in chapter one, even these systems relate in some way to time, or worker activity in specific cases.

In all schemes it is evident that the major disadvantages are to do with the concept of measuring per se. The limitations are threefold. First, social work contains components which are to some extent indefinable and therefore immeasurable. These are to do with both the variability of the worker and the variability of the task. Second, social workers work at different speeds, or certain situations make different demands on them as individuals. This variable is perhaps more consistent than the unpredictability of any given case. Finally, the pervasiveness of the social work task which makes it both more rewarding and more demanding than many other professions, also makes it difficult to measure. Whether a hair trigger precision measurement of workloads is possible, relates to whether they are desirable (Orme, 1989). Chapter 1 has outlined the benefits for organisations and workers which can accrue from having an effective workload scheme. It explored briefly whether this effectiveness derived solely from a system of measurement, or whether management involvement in the process of monitoring workloads was significant. This discussion about the function of workload systems and the uses to which they are put is developed further in Chapter 6.

The research project

At the time that the motion was passed at the NAPO annual general meeting there had been no initiative from the Home Office to update PSWM, and the received wisdom was that there were no plans for revisions in the future. A study of the application of the PSWM to probation workloads had been undertaken previously (Glastonbury et al, 1987), and this provided the basis for negotiations with NAPO to undertake research to investigate some of the issues in workload measurement raised by the earlier study, which were congruent with the concerns of probation officers voiced at their annual conference.

The focus would be on a discrete task in order to test the notion of a workload measure. While focusing on the activity of individual probation officers, the aim would be to attempt to capture all of the input by the probation officer into a particular activity, irrespective of how that activity was defined. It was assumed that this would lead to a more accurate time per task measurement. While the desired outcome for NAPO was to challenge the actual timings allocated under the PSWM, it was anticipated that the research would also highlight the process of capturing activity. These findings might contribute to refining existing systems. Alternatively, they might challenge the feasibility of operating workload measuring systems with any degree of accuracy.

The task of preparing a social inquiry (SIR) was chosen for a variety of reasons. First, it is a discrete task which makes it accessible for the purposes of measurement. Second, in the description of the task in the previous chapter, links have been made between this as an assessment process and parallel tasks in other social work agencies. Finally, the SIR has particular significance for the work of the probation service and in debates on workload measurement systems to date. The reasons for this include:

1 In the working party set up to oversee the weightings which emerged from the 1978 PSWM study, the allocation of time for the task of preparing an SIR had been the most hotly disputed weighting - and the only one which was changed after pressure from NAPO.

2 In the evaluation of the application of the weightings (Glastonbury et al 1987), it was the allocation for the SIR which was challenged consistently by probation officers on the grounds of not giving them time to do the job properly.

3 Reports for the court are seen as crucial documents by the service, demanding professional expertise. The assessment informs other work and influences who is put on probation. Report writing is experienced as a stressful activity because of the need to work to deadlines and the

involvement in making recommendations which can effect people's liberty. This high profile is equally true for the preparation of the Pre-Sentence Reports (PSRs) introduced by the 1991 Criminal Justice Act. It is assumed that whatever changes occur within the probation service as a result of policy initiatives,there will always be a role for expert report writing.

4 Because there are a number of consumers or stakeholders involved in the preparation of a social inquiry report there are a variety of ways in which effectiveness can be judged.

5 There are a set of standards against which the document prepared could be evaluated, to assess whether best practice had been followed. The Home Office Circular (92/1986) gave specific guidelines on purpose, structure and content of SIRs which has significance for the activity levels of officers preparing the reports.

A research project to follow the preparation of individual SIRs would therefore enable all the work of a particular activity to be captured, with individual probation officers recording all the activity connected with each report. This was seen to be necessary because, in debating the motion at the AGM, officers had reported giving time to SIR preparation by thinking about particular reports while driving the car or lying in the bath. While it might not be possible to give appropriate weighting to all such activity, this debate highlighted the need to track as much activity as possible related to individual cases, in order to reflect the demands on individual workers.

Such distinctions are important because, apart from workload measurement projects initiated by the Home Office there had been one other related study, undertaken in the 1970s (Davies and Knopf, 1973). Although focusing on the task of preparing court reports, the authors of this study were clear that it was not concerned with quality or effectiveness of the work undertaken, but how much time was spent on the task, and how that time is distributed. Nevertheless, it provides interesting points of comparison for the study described in this text.

Design

The intention of the research project therefore was to do more than log the time per task spent on preparing social inquiry reports. Merely to replicate the earlier projects would not meet the criticisms which had been raised. Additionally, it was not intended to undertake large scale data collection. The issues that had been raised by probation staff were about the complexity of the social work task and the difficulties of encapsulating, or accurately calculating this, in a workload measurement system. While some notion of time had to been included, the aim was to enable those involved in the process of writing the reports, and those for whom the reports had been prepared, to give some evaluation of the standard of these reports. This evaluation would not only be of the final document, but would include an assessment of the process. It might then be possible to identify whether those reports which were deemed to be useful and effective did take more time to prepare, or whether other factors affected the time taken in a particular task, and the standard to which it was performed.

The aim was to produce a descriptive research project in the evaluative tradition (Powell & Lovelock, 1992). The reasons for this are manifold. First, the relevance of a positivist position that there could be an absolute definition of either the task of report writing in social work, or the time that should be taken to undertake such tasks, is questioned. As has been outlined in Chapter 1, the adoption of workload measurements in social work, or indeed in any human resource activity, is of limited value as an absolute exercise and can only be effective within a broader project of positive management. The dangers and pitfalls of seeing workload measurement as an precise science are further explored in Chapter 6, but at this stage it is important to assert that the project was not about precision measurement. The resistance of social workers to research projects which merely reflected a managerial approach to data collection with its inspectorial overtones have already been documented (Goldberg & Fruin, 1976, Everitt et al., 1994) and meant that such an approach was to be avoided. Indeed the fact that the research was in part funded by a trade union/professional association meant that the identification with managerial approaches was unlikely, but the rhetoric of conditions of service can be equally positivistic and constraining. The research had to provide appropriate and relevant information to be useful in debates which were taking place between the NAPO and management, but this had to be acquired rigorously. The commitment was to ensure the appropriate factors were considered for the working conditions of probation officers, but also to the quality of the service which would ultimately be offered to the offenders for whom the service was provided, and indeed the tax payers who were funding the service.

Equally, in disseminating the research results, notice had to be taken of Goldberg and Fruin's warning that 'much of evaluative experimental research on the effectiveness of social work has been carried out in atypical situations' (1976, p5) which meant that studies were not able to be replicated, and the results could therefore be dismissed as unverifiable. The assumption here is that other research methodologies reflect typical situations and that experiences are able to be repeated. The aims of this research were to enable those involved in the process give their views, and to attempt to identify all the influences on the process of preparing a court report which ultimately affected the time taken to complete the task. The circumstances of each report would be different, and the overall process would be influenced by being part of a research project, this is equally true of research carried out in any tradition, the very process of researching an event makes it untypical. These aims would be met by using a variety of methodologies. The research therefore had three main components:

Measuring the time per task. This involved collecting data on the activity of preparing social enquiry reports and the time that was spent both on the total process of preparing the document, and on the component parts.

Probation officers would be asked to keep a log of activities involved in preparing reports. At a simple level this would provide a comparison with the weightings allocated to preparing reports in the 1972 and 1978 exercises. These weightings involved a time measure, a record of time spent on all activities to do with preparing the report. However, the collection of data on time would go beyond this. A breakdown of all activities involved in the preparation of the reports would be made, and the time spent on the component parts would be logged. This would assist officers to log the total time, but would also identify the whole range of activities in which a reporting officer might be involved. This would create a wealth of data about some of the highly individualistic practices involved in report writing, but might give some guidelines on what processes could be streamlined, and which are seen to be effective. Such data would also give information about the use of professional time in a variety of activities which might otherwise be classified as administrative and clerical. Furthermore, there were repeated debates in the probation service about whether the attendance of probation officers at court was an effective use of time. Such attendances often involved individual officers in long waiting times, because their time was seen to be less important (and less expensive) than that of members of the legal profession.

To facilitate the collection of data on timings a pro forma would be designed to ensure there was some consistent collection of data on activities, but this would be flexible enough to allow officers to record any additional or unusual activity connected with the preparation of specific reports. This phase of the research, the request that officers log how much time they spent on each stage of preparing a report, obviously made officers more conscious of being involved in a research project and this could affect practice. Officers might spend more time, be more assiduous, because they knew they were being observed, or more accurately their activities were being recorded. This was precisely the aim of this part of the research, and had been built in to measure time taken by those attempting to achieve best professional practice as laid down in the guidelines. This might counteract the criticism of NARS that officers tried to demonstrate how busy they were, and therefore completed many tasks very quickly. NARS did not attempt to measure effectiveness.

The output. In order to make comparisons between all the possible variables which might affect the time it took to prepare a report, information relating to the officer preparing the report would be collected and details about the preparing the report and the circumstances of the offender on whom the report was prepared would be logged.

In the initial stages of setting up the project all participating officers would be asked to complete a pro forma which would record basic information such as age, sex, ethnic origin and length of service. Other information such as type of training and whether they were in a specialist court team or a generic team were also logged. There were specific reasons for including such data. At the time the research was undertaken the probation service had a fully qualified probation officer workforce and an unqualified staff group who were designated Ancillaries (this group is now called Probation Assistants). SIRs were written only be qualified probation officers. There was a single professional qualification, the Certificate in Qualification for Social Work (CQSW), but a dual route by either a one year postgraduate or a two-year non-graduate course. In view of the suggestion that probation officers might vary in their approach to tasks and their workload capacity it may be that type of training would influence this.

Similarly there was speculation that the organisation of the work might influence the time spent on particular tasks. For example, officers working in a specialist court team and spending their total working time might have access to information more easily than officers holding generic workloads and preparing only occasional reports. There may, for example, be special systems to ensure information from the police (eg antecedent histories of the offenders) or the courts (eg depositions in crown court cases) were routinely available when a case was allocated. This would cut down on the administrative burden on the report writers. Alternatively, long term involvement in court work, which was acknowledged to be highly stressed, might lead to burnout and the production of less effective reports (Glastonbury et al, 1987).

Similarly, the collection of data about individual offenders on whom reports were written was designed to capture other variables which might affect the time spent on report preparation. These include type of offence, offending history, sex, age and ethnic background. There was also speculation that aspects of the offenders lifestyle might affect the amount of time that was spent preparing the report. For example, the employment status of the offender might be relevant. The suggestion was that, during the preparation of SIRs, probation officers might intervene and use social work skills to enable individuals to access resources. Such intervention might be used to divert from a custodial sentence, or alleviate the need for some form of supervision. Obviously, if probation officers were working with individuals searching for employment, this would be more time consuming than merely checking the record of someone in employment.

Differences in the intervention patterns of probation officer might relate to offenders who were homeless and required help finding accommodation. Finally, while offenders remanded in custody might be more accessible for interview, the officer might need to negotiate with a number of agencies to provide an effective plan for a non-custodial sentence.

In order to capture this information the author of the report would complete a pro forma detailing the offenders situation. In addition the researcher would receive a copy of every report prepared and would complete a questionnaire based on the report and information provided by the reporting officer. This would obviously provide cross checking, and the completed form could be used as part of the evaluation of the SIR.

Evaluation

Evaluation could come from a variety of sources, some of which relate to research undertaken on social inquiry reports which has been described in the previous chapter. In addition, the system for evaluating the reports should reflect the fact that there are a number of consumers of reports and that it would be invaluable to have consumer feedback on specific reports.

a) Self assessment by the author of the report. In the first instance there would be a self assessment completed by the officer preparing the report. This would involve a statement of satisfaction, and, in recognition that the aim of the research was to identify the time it might take to perform a task to the best possible standard, an opportunity to state what factors had influenced the self-evaluation. In the light of the particular constraints of preparing SIRs for the court, which include time limits and deadlines, a particular question about time constraints would be asked. This would include actual time constraints such as short remands, but also an acknowledgement that at any one time when a report has to be prepared there are other demands on a probation officers time. Reports are not prepared in a vacuum.

b) Sentencers. SIRs were written specifically to assist the court come to a decision about the appropriate sentence for individual offenders. It was originally planned that there would be a system of obtaining the views of individual sentencers on particular reports. While this might be time consuming, in that different Magistrates sit on the bench on different days of the week and they would have to be informed about the research and they would need to be followed up to ascertain there views on reports, it was thought to be important. However, in the very early stages of setting up the research it became apparent that, for a variety of reasons, it would be difficult to get permission to access the sentencers. Despite best efforts to negotiate access the Lord Chancellor's Department was resistant to any approach being made to the judiciary and Clerks to the Justices were protective of magistrates.

In the absence of direct access to sentencers, it was decided to do a two stage assessment to try and gauge sentencers satisfaction. In the first instance a question was included in the form for the probation officers writing the report, asking if the court requested any further information. It was likely that this would only be requested if the sentencers were dissatisfied with the information presented in the reports.

A further evaluation of sentencer satisfaction is reflected in the take up of recommendations in reports by the sentencers (Ford, 1972; Thorpe and Pease, 1976). This information is simply collected by logging the recommendation and the sentence. To this end the probation officer questionnaires included independent questions about recommendations and sentence which would enable an analysis to be made of the rate of take up of recommendations. This could be double checked by reading the report to identify the recommendation, and the sentence could be checked from the central records. The data could be analyzed to identify the percentage take up of recommendations and the findings compared to other studies. The consensus of previous research is that a range from 63% (Stanley and Murphy, 1984) to 80% (Ford, 1972) take up of recommendations could be expected. Having said that, it is possible to question take up of recommendation as a direct assessment of the total quality of the report. The notion of 'second guessing', that is a process by which probation officers will make recommendations because they are operating according to some form of sentencing tariff, or because they are alert to the sentencing behaviour of particular judges and magistrates, could influence recommendations, rather than an assumption that the sentencers were persuaded by the quality of the report prepared. Alternatively, it may be that there is concordance in the assessment of both sentencers and report writers. However, acknowledging these limitations, it was thought relevant to ascertain whether the take up of recommendations in this sample related to other studies.

c) Offender evaluation. In any evaluation of SIRs an important consequence is the effect on the offender. As the subject of the SIR, and as the recipient of the sentence which is passed, the offender is therefore and important stakeholder in the production of the SIR, and in all aspects of the process of its production. It was therefore seen as important to canvas the opinion of offenders on the quality of the experience of the production of the SIR. However, because of the investment in the outcome of the process it was decided that to evaluate offender reaction at the point of sentence might monitor a reaction to the sentence rather than the experience of having an SIR prepared. It was therefore decided to contact offenders some six months after sentence so that a retrospective view of the process of having the SIR prepared could be incorporated.

Conclusion

This chapter has described the initial stages of setting up a research project to monitor the workloads involved for probation officers in preparing reports for the criminal courts. At the time of the research these reports were called social inquiry reports (SIRs). The aim was to address criticisms which had been made of other studies to capture probation officers workloads, which were that they concentrated on time taken without any consideration of the quality of the work undertaken. In describing the background to the specific piece of research issues of methodology are discussed, and reference is made to the specific factors which impinge upon researching in the court setting. In particular, when considering issues of quality, the involvement of stakeholders in the research process is essential.

4 Negotiating the research

Introduction

This chapter contains a detailed account of specific issues relating to setting up a research project to identify how long it took probation ofciers to prepare a social inquiry report, when they were attempting to ensure that they undertook the task according to their understanding of best professional practice. The parameters of the research, including decisions about research methods and personnel to be involved, will be documented. The process of engaging subjects will be outlined, and ethical dilemmas and practical arrangements described. The account will give the background to the results described in the next chapter.

Negotiating the research

It was envisaged that the research would be undertaken on the report writing practices of probation officers in two different probation services. This would ensure that the results would reflect the ways in which different services might interpret legislation and policy guidelines relating to the preparation of court reports. Also, different geographical areas would ensure that different patterns of offending behaviour would be represented. While there was no attempt to have representative samples of offenders or offences, it was an underlying principle that the research would acknowledge the gender and ethnic composition of offending populations. Such an approach is seen to reflect good research practice (Orme and Forbes, 1991). To this end it was decided to approach probation areas where there was more likelihood of offenders from ethnic minority backgrounds being represented in the sample.

Different probation areas would also reflect different ways of organising and managing the tasks to be undertaken. In the earlier work on applying workload measurement (Glastonbury et al, 1987), it had become apparent that the existence of a specialist court team influenced the task of preparing reports in a number of ways. In view of this, it was decided that one team of probation officers would represent specialist teams who provided a service to the courts, and whose workload consisted almost entirely of writing reports for the courts. The second team would be a 'generic' team which meant that they would be supervising offenders on orders from the court, but would write occasional reports, usually on those currently under supervision, but also for those who had previously been under supervision. Report writing for this team would not be specialist activity, but they would have regular contact with the courts.

It took some time to negotiate the data collection systems. Initially two probation teams were identified. They were chosen after some discussions with representatives of NAPO because they met the criteria identified. The teams chosen:

1 Represented the different functional organisation of the service. One team was a specialist court team and the second prepared SIRs as part of their generic workload.

2 Were in different probation areas and represented different populations. In particular one team was chosen because it represented an area with a greater number of ethnic minority groups within its population.

In addition both teams were accessible to the researcher, but were distant from each other and represented very different management structures.

In the first instance both teams were approached by NAPO to ascertain whether they would be willing, in principle, to participate in the research. Once an agreement in principle had been given, permission was sought from the Association of Chief Officers of Probation by NAPO for the research to be undertaken. Once there were positive indications, the Chief Probation Officers of the areas concerned were contacted and the aims of the research outlined. Meetings were arranged in the two areas to discuss the research further. Discussions with the individual chief officers included clarification of the research aims and the extent of the involvement of the service. The researcher received information about the management and policy initiatives within the two services to confirm that there was nothing which might make these teams untypical. At this point there was no suggestion that there was a 'typical' probation team, but clarification was sought that there was nothing dramatically different which might influence either the preparation of reports, or the level of probation input. Assurances were sought that the teams were not likely to be subject to major changes during the anticipated period of the research. Finally, it was ascertained that these teams had not been involved in any related research in the recent past. The concern here was not that officers would be contaminated by research, but that they might be research-weary.

Once permission was gained at managerial level, approaches were made to the team leaders and arrangements made for the researcher to meet with the team members. Initial meetings took place to outline the research and discuss broad issues. The teams were then asked to discuss the project over time and inform the researcher whether they were willing to participate. If there was agreement further meetings would take place to discuss the practicalities of the research. During the period of decision making there were a series of delays caused primarily by changes in the leadership of one of the teams. It was thought that this change would not have too great an effect on the teams participation, but the contract had to be re-negotiated with the new team leader.

Pilot study

While the negotiations were taking place to obtain the co-operation of the probation services to set up the research, a pilot study was undertaken in an area which was not to be a pilot site for the main study. This involved the researcher, an ex-probation officer, undertaking the preparation of a sample set of reports for the local Probation Office. These reports were chosen to represent both crown and magistrates court reports and included male and female offenders. All reports were on offenders who were not currently on supervision, although they may have had previous experience of supervision. In all six reports were prepared.

Such an arrangement, while contributing to the research design raises the first of the ethical questions. While agreement was reached that the researcher could be accredited by the agency to undertake the task, there were obvious issues of accountability. The model chosen was therefore along the lines of a trainee social worker on a practice placement. Each report was allocated and supervised by a Senior Probation Officer who ensured the quality of the service to the individuals on whom the reports were prepared. Supervision sessions were accompanied by discussions for the purpose of the research, exploring related aspects of preparing social inquiry reports which might impinge upon the research process.

During the pilot a log was prepared of all the activities related to the process of preparing reports. The log included notes about particular circumstances which might influence the time spent on these activities.

53

For example, the researcher's lack of recent experience meant that when a report required attendance at the Crown Court time was spent with the Crown Court Liaison Officer preparing for the appearance. Such preparation might also be relevant to officers who worked in an area where report writing was a specialist function and officers involved in supervising offenders made few appearances in the Crown Court. A particular report, involving a serious sex offence, was also a vivid reminder for the researcher of the sense of responsibility that accompanies writing reports on offenders whose offences have impinged significantly upon the lives of others, and who are at risk of custody. This served to reinforce the need for the evaluative comments from officers on the process of writing reports.

Various methods of monitoring the time spent on the component activities were attempted. In particular, attention was given to the need to capture all the work involved in the preparation of the report, whoever undertook this work. For example, a report which involved an assessment for community service involved activities by the reporting officer in arranging for the assessment and liaising about the recommendations. While there was also time spent by other members of the service interviewing the defendant and contacting possible projects, these were not captured in the time reporting. The aim was to try and identify how much time a reporting officer would spend on the particular task. Workload measurement for other purposes, i.e staffing levels in the service, would need to capture the total workload.

At the end of the pilot study the questionnaires and other documentation for completion by the probation officers had been designed and refined. These were then taken to the teams who had agreed to participate in the research, to see if local conditions would influence either the information collected or the process of collection.

Consultation with the teams

Once the teams had given their agreement to participate there were a series of meetings between the researcher and each team. In the first instance feedback on the research process was sought, and specific response to the emerging questionnaires and other relevant documentation was requested.

The first change was to the document listing the activities involved in preparing a report. The specialist court team had a consultation stage built into the process of preparation. This was significant because it was an early implementation of a gatekeeping system, which later became NAPO policy and is now an integral part of national standards for the probation service in preparing PSRs (Home Office, 1992). Gatekeeping fulfils a number of functions. It ensures that probation officers are not making inappropriate recommendations which might precipitate offenders into custody, and it has been used in connection with programmes for targeting offenders who might be at risk of custody, but who might be diverted effectively. As such, gatekeeping was seen to reflect good probation practice and incorporated good equal opportunities practice, by ensuring that racist and sexist language and stereotypes were not used in the reports. This introduction of gatekeeping would obviously affect the time devoted to the process of preparing an SIR and a section was added to the questionnaire to allow for this to be recorded appropriately.

A major discussion occurred around the notion of consent. Which highlights a second ethical issue. The focus of the research was probation officers' activity, and their consent was essential. The discussions about the process of the research raised little concern, although it was acknowledged that participating in the research would add to the workloads of the officers involved. The irony of this was acknowledged, that research to identify and acknowledge workload pressures would be adding to those pressures, but it was acknowledged that it was inescapable. At this point in the negotiations the involvement and support of NAPO was seen to be significant. The concern therefore was not that there would be bias in the research, but that the interpretation and application of the results might be seen to redress what had previously been seen as a managerial initiative.

However, even the involvement of NAPO did not allay all concerns. Officers expressed some apprehension about the destination of the results, especially the evaluation of the quality of the report writing process. This reflected an issue raised in early work on workloads (Goldberg and Fruin, 1976), that practitioner co-operation in research is limited because of negative experiences. Often social workers are involved in data collection for a number of purposes, but the end results are not made clear. There is, therefore, a need to build into any research process the opportunity to feedback the results to the participants. This is seen to be best practice, and goes some way to meeting criticisms that research acquires information about people's experience, and then reframes that experience according to some theoretical framework (Croft and Beresford, 1986). There was understandable concern that if information was made available to management about the performance of individual officers, this might be used for other purposes. Obviously this was not acceptable to those participating, and failure to protect those participating would lead either to their lack of cooperation, or would mean that they would be less open in their self assessment. It was important to give assurances that there would be protection for those participating. Information would only be given about aggregated data and no officer would be identifiable. All information would be recorded using a coding system for both officers and reports, which would be known only to the researcher. Conversely, some team members indicated that they would be interested in receiving individual feedback, especially from those on whom the reports were prepared. However, it was thought that anonymity should also be guaranteed to those who agreed to participate and it was not possible to give individual feedback.

The involvement of the defendants upon whom the reports were prepared led to further concerns. It was planned that defendants on whom rpeorts were prepared would be contacted for their evaluative comments. It was envisaged that their consent would be sought at the point that feedback was requested, they would be contacted by letter and asked if they wished to participate. Concern was expressed by the members of one team about issues of consent of those on whom the reports were being prepared, suggesting that it should be obtained at the point of preparation of the report. It had been assumed that because they were not the prime focus of the research, there would not be any need to obtain the consent of the offenders, the subjects of the reports, for the first part of the study. Although SIRs are not in the public domain, details of offenders and offences are, and it was not intended to use information other than that which could be publicly available. For the later stages of the research, the feedback from offenders about the experience of having the report prepared, it was apparent that appropriate approaches would have to be made.

The team raising the issues suggested that at the point that the report was prepared offenders should be asked to give their consent. It was pointed out that the report was about their experience, and as such they should have a say in their involvement. In addition, the inclusion of that report in the research meant that they would be contacted at a later stage for feedback on the process, although at that point they could refuse to be involved. A letter some months after the court appearance might have a significant affect. Circumstances may have changed, and they might not wish to be reminded of the offence. There was also a risk that a letter might reveal the existence of a criminal record when the defendant had wished to keep this concealed.

While the ethical dilemma was acknowledged, it raised practical complications. Suggestions that the reporting officer should inform the defendant about the research and ask for their consent were thought to be impractical. To do this would introduce factors which were extraneous to the process of writing the report. It could lead to a debate about the research and the consequences of being involved in it. All of this would occur in an interview for the purposes of preparing a report, and would be logged as time involved in preparing the report. This dilemma was put to the other probation team and was discussed with significant others to establish a view on the ethics of the responsibility of the researcher to all of those involved in the research.

It was resolved that a written statement would be prepared which would be handed to the subjects of the reports once the report had been

56

completed. Individuals who did not wish to be contacted for the feedback stage could be identified and they would not be involved in the research. Alternatively, arrangements could be made for contact to be made through, for example, the report writer. This was thought to be particularly significant where the outcome of the court appearance for which the report was prepared was a prison sentence.

Finally, the discussions with the teams also addressed the ways in which contact could be made with those involved in sentencing. Specific contact people were given for the two magistrates courts for which most of the report writing was undertaken. However the teams indicated that they wrote reports for a number of other courts and that the task of receiving feedback on every report would be extremely complex and, given the limited resources, impractical. It was agreed to focus on the courts for whom most reports were written. However, in the final analysis, despite strenuous efforts it was not possible to negotiate the involvement of the magistrates and judges.

The research process

The collection of information on the process of preparing SIRs occurred between 17th April to 26th May 1989. This period equated to a calendar month but began and ended mid-month to avoid the Easter and Spring Bank Holidays. It did include a one day May Day holiday but this was thought not to disrupt workloads significantly.

The period of a month was chosen because both areas indicated that there would be a substantial number of reports completed in that period and it is acknowledged in workload measurement research that the rate of documenting the necessary information drops off rapidly over time. As the research was not a quantitative study there was no imperative to set a target number of reports, to try and attain a representative sample. The aim was to collect as much data as possible about the preparation of reports in a given period by two probation teams. The process of collating all the information for the purposes of the research was slightly different for each team.

Team A: Court Team

This team was the specialist team who prepared reports on defendants appearing in magistrates and crown courts which they serviced.
It was agreed that officers would complete a questionnaire on all reports prepared during this period on defendants who were not already on supervision. These questionnaires, together with a copy of the report, would be lodged with the court team secretary. The researcher would then collect the documentation from the office and chase up any stragglers.

In order to capture all the reports prepared during the research period it was necessary to allow at least three weeks after the completion of data collection to allow for the remand period of any reports allocated from magistrates at the end of the research period. Crown Court reports were likely to take considerably longer than a month to be dealt with and there were trawls at later dates to capture all the information relating to these.

It was apparent at the first collection that officers had not been assiduous in completing questionnaires or lodging them and the SIR. Reminders were sent out and further collections were undertaken in July and September.

A total of thirty eight questionnaires were collected at the end of all the searches. A check of the allocation book showed that ninety one reports had been allocated during the period and, as this was a court team, the reports allocated were unlikely to be on offenders currently under supervision. It could therefore be expected that data about activity and time would have been collected on the preparation of the majority of these reports.

This obviously had not occurred and there is no apparent rationale for officers' decisions to complete questionnaires. The two officers with the highest number of reports allocated succeeded in completing a good proportion (one third in one case and a half in another.) It is difficult to comment on whether officers chose to complete questionnaires on the most difficult and/or the most time consuming reports, but it is possible that those that were more demanding of time were less likely to be included in the sample because officers would not be bothered to fill in a questionnaire alongside all the other activity.

Only one officer from Team A had attached an SIR to the relevant questionnaire. A search of central records was undertaken for three sets of information:

1 The completed report so that a copy could be attached to the data file for further analysis.

2 Confirmation of the sentence imposed by the court.

3 The current address of the offender so that a questionnaire could be sent out to all defendants who had a report prepared and an officer questionnaire had been completed. All questionnaires were included in this exercise.

The initial information collection was completed during October so that questionnaires to defendants could be sent out in November. This was some six months after the commencement of the initial data collection. It was thought to be far enough away from the court appearance to avoid answers being totally influenced by the outcome of the court appearance, i.e. the sentence, rather than the process of the report being written. It should also ensure that any crown court appearances would be completed and the outcome known - if this had been holding up the completion of some officer questionnaires.

Team B: Generic team

This team undertook supervision of offenders on orders from the Court. They prepared reports when those whom they were supervising committed further offences. In addition, because there was no specialist court team in their area, they prepared court reports on defendants who were appearing before the courts for the first time, or who were not previously known to the probation service.

This team completed the data collection as required and attached a copy of the SIR to the relevant questionnaire therefore all the information was readily available. The total number of reports allocated during the survey period (six allocation days) was forty two. There were fourteen questionnaires completed on reports allocated during this period. This low return was explained in terms of the team having completed a high number of reports on individuals already known to them. One officer had reports allocated throughout the survey period only on offenders known to him, and therefore completed no questionnaires. Also, the team only completed questionnaires on reports prepared on defendants appearing before the local courts.

Questionnaires to defendants

The total number of defendants upon whom questionnaires had been completed was fifty two, of whom forty eight had an address. One defendant was of no fixed address (NFA) at the time of sentence and the record card had no contact address. Three had been sentenced to periods of imprisonment which would mean that they were still in custody. A decision was made that, where the sentence was relatively short, the defendant was likely to be in the local prison and the questionnaire was sent directly to the one person in this category. The other two both had probation officers allocated to them and questionnaires were sent to those probation officers for onward transmission.

In the light of the ethical issues discussed above, about the involvement of the defendants in the follow up, one defendant had indicated that he did not want a follow up questionnaire sent to his home address. It was agreed that the questionnaire would be sent to the probation officer, if there was still voluntary contact. The defendant would then consider completing it.

A letter explaining the research was sent to forty seven defendants at addresses recorded in the probation filing systems. Included was a questionnaire asking for feedback on the experience of having the report prepared and a stamped addressed envelope.

Initially eleven offender questionnaires were returned, of which one was returned address unknown. A second had been forwarded to a new address, the questionnaire completed and new address was supplied. A further follow up was undertaken, which included a first request to the defendant on whom information had just been received. A total of seventeen offender evaluations were eventually received.

Independent evaluation

Eventually forty three complete sets of data were then collated. The absence of evaluation from the magistrates and judges meant that a further stage of evaluation needed to be constructed. It was thought important to have an independent evaluation, conducted by someone who was not a stakeholder. As a former probation officer and a tutor on a social work training course with special responsibility for probation students, the researcher had knowledge of the necessary criteria for the preparation of an SIR. This knowledge had been reinforced by the pilot study. It was therefore decided that, in addition to the various forms, a copy of the SIR prepared would be evaluated by the researcher. It was also acknowledged that an assessment based on a simple reading of the reports might merely be an expression of subjective opinion. To provide a more systematic framework for the evaluation the Home Office circular 92/1986 was used, especially the section on *The Structure and Content of SIRs*. The guidelines contained were particularly significant because they acknowledged the amount of probation officer time involved in preparing reports, and that the benefits of good practice in that 'a well written SIR can be of great assistance to the court and have significant influence on what happens to an offender' (1986, p1), thus encapsulating the various strands of the research.

The circular identified good practice by recommneding that a report should identify sources; the writer should provide details of the offender's criminal history and a copy of the report should be given to the defendant or the defendant's counsel or solicitor. While there was no general rule given about the length of a report it was suggested that 'reports which are concise and well-expressed are likely to be heeded more readily' and guidance that they should be 'as short as possible while still covering the main points' (1986, p5). In stating that an SIR 'should contain information about the defendant's personality and character, and, in order to seek explanation for the offending behaviour should set the defendant in his or her social circumstances', the circular lists ten areas to be considered. In addition, special attention was drawn to the need to evaluate the defendant's attitude to the offence; significant aspects of the defendant's social or cultural background in cases where s/he was a member of ethnic minorities (sic). Finally, SIR writers were recommended to provide particular information, where this was requested by the court and to offer an assessment of 'how far and by what means the offender might be encouraged or assisted not to repeat his or her offending behaviour' (Home Office, 1986, p8), which would include a review of sentencing options.

These guidelines were incorporated into a *Social Inquiry Report Questionnaire,* which was completed using a coding frame. This culminated in a score for each report being given and on the basis of theses scores reports were classified as poor, satisfactory, good or excellent.

Conclusion

This chapter has described in some detail the process of setting up a research project to identify the time taken to undertake the variety of activities undertaken by probation officers in the preparation of reports for the criminal courts. This process included undertaking a pilot study, negotiating the research at a number of levels, and collecting the data. In describing all the stages, particular attention has been drawn to issues of involving practitioners in research projects. These issues include discussions about how the context of the research may influence both the process and the outcome. This is particularly significant when the research is attempting to both measure and assess direct work with clients or users of social work agencies. The fact that the context is complex, as is the task, means that there is no one single method of undertaking the research which will provide the necessary information. The decision about the use of different methods is therefore explored.

Also, researching social work practice inevitably raises a number of ethical issues, in that focus is on the very private areas of individuals lives. The chapter therefore draws attention to specific ethical issues which were raised during this project. Finally, although agreement was obtained at the outset, a number of factors impinge upon those involved in research during the process. These are documented in some detail, again in the hope that they will add to an understanding of the complexities of researching social work practice.

5 Court reports and workload measurement

Introduction

This chapter describes the results of the research. It includes detailed information relating to the time logged by probation officers for performing the task of preparing social inquiry reports. In producing these results it becomes evident that it is not possible to provide hair trigger precision timings. The aim is therefore to analyze what factors influence the time taken to prepare reports. More importantly, the evaluation of the reports prepared will give information about the quality of the reports. Qualitative material provided by worker and offender respondents will be used to identify issues for the process of workload measurement and its contribution to management.

In the course of collecting this data it was also possible to capture the various tasks associated with producing a court report, assessed against the expectations of the Home Office, as reflected in an official circular (92/1986). These recommendations have now been superseded by national standards (Home Office, 1992) which refer to the preparation of pre-sentence reports. They therefore reflect differing expectations, not because the task is substantially different, but the management culture of the probation service has changed significantly. This chapter provides a link between the description of the results pertaining to the original purpose of the research, to explore the time taken to prepare SIRs according to best professional standards and an analysis of the changes in the uses of workload measurement in management systems.

Description of the sample

A description of those involved in this project provides important background material. In terms of subjects or sample, the research has two major sets of actors, the officers who were involved in preparing the reports and the defendants upon whom the reports were prepared.

Writers of the reports

Probation officers in the teams during the research period included six officers from Team A (the specialist court team) and seven from Team B (the generic team). All but one officer was a basic grade probation officer. The senior probation officer in Team B was included because he occasionally wrote reports. One officer in Team A had a specially designated role of Crown Court Liaison Officer. Team B had only two female probation officers, while Team A comprised four women and two men. One officer self-described as Afro-Caribbean and another as African. All the others described themselves as white.

Four of the officers were over the age of forty years, all the rest being between ages of twenty four and forty years, with the majority of the reports being prepared by officers under thirty years of age. Although only six of the participating officers were in their first five years of service, the majority of the reports in the sample were written by these officers. This does not mean that these officers were more likely to be allocated reports, but that officers closer to training were are likely to be interested in participating in research. One officer had undertaken a four year degree leading to a social work qualification, while three other officers had undertaken training which had not been sponsored by the Home Office. All the other participating officers had been trained on postgraduate courses and had been sponsored by the Home Office for specific training for the probation service.

Although this was the broad composition of the officers in the participating teams, in fact three officers did not produce any material for the research. One officer was on leave during most of the period and did not have reports allocated on their return, and in the case of the senior probation officer no reports were allocated. The third officer simply did not complete any of the questionnaires related to report writing, even though reports were allocated during the period and agreement about participation had been reached with all members of the team. The reason for this non-participation was that the officer had been too busy during the period to undertake extra paperwork.

Of the forty three complete sets of research information twenty nine (67%) related to reports prepared by Team A (the court team) and fourteen (33%) to reports from Team B. This split is to be expected as officers in a specialist court team are, by definition, preparing more court reports than those in generic teams. However the proportion of reports prepared on which research material was collected was greater for Team B. This may be because officers in the court team frequently have to produce additional paperwork for the courts, for prisons or for other officers in the service. Logging of timings for the purposes of research may have felt like an additional burden.

Subjects of the reports

While a total of twelve reports were prepared on females and thirty one reports (72%) on males. It is difficult to establish whether this in line with the general statistics on social inquiry reports, because those for 1989 do not give a gender breakdown (Home Office, 1990c).

Although there had been an attempt to build into the research the opportunity to analyze the service to offenders from backgrounds other than white British, the sample produced little opportunity to do this. The majority of the reports, thirty five, were prepared on offenders who were described as being of white United Kingdom (UK) origin. Five reports were prepared on offenders described as being of European origin, and three on offenders described as being of Irish origin. As there was no ethnic monitoring of offenders in place in the criminal justice system at the time of the research it is difficult to make any comparisons with other data.

In terms of age, the largest cluster of offenders appeared in the seventeen to twenty years age range. There were thirteen reports (30%) reports written on offenders in this age range, of whom nine were male and four female. This was the largest grouping for male offenders and constituted 29% of all males in the sample, and 21% of the total sample. The second largest age grouping for males was twenty one to twenty five years of age. There were eight reports prepared on male offenders in this group, which constituted 26% of all males in the sample, and 19% of the total sample.

However for reports on females, marginally the largest grouping was reports on women between the ages of thirty one and forty years. Five reports were prepared on females in this age range.

Of the total number of reports, thirty one (72%) were prepared for magistrates Court, and twelve (28%) were prepared for crown court. Only one of the crown court reports was written on a female offender. At the time the reports were prepared thirty seven defendants were on bail, and this included all the women on whom reports were prepared. One report was prepared on a defendant who was in a bail hostel, and the remaining five reports were prepared on defendants who were in custody.

Offences

Documenting offences in the preparation of social inquiry reports is complicated because offenders are often dealt with for more than one offence at the court hearing, although reports may not always mention all offences. For the purposes of this study, which was focusing on report writing, offences were analyzed either by the one mentioned by the report writer or, where there were multiple offences referenced in the report, the most serious was logged. In that there were only forty three reports in the sample, and the distribution of offenders across all offences is usually quite wide, the numbers for each become quite small. The following table identifies the distribution of offences against the sex of the offender.

Table 5.1
Offences committed by offenders in the sample

Offence	Females	Males	Total
Theft	3	6	9
Assault	2	4	6
Deception	1	3	4
Robbery	0	2	2
Excess alcohol	0	2	2
Burglary	1	4	5
Shoplifting	0	4	4
Possession	1	0	1
Fraud	4	0	4
Criminal damage	0	1	1
Disqualif. driving	0	2	2
GBH	0	1	1
Take & drive away	0	1	1
Rape	0	1	1
Indecent exposure	0	1	1
Total	**12**	**31**	**43**

Time taken to prepare reports

The starting point for analyzing the time taken to write reports in this sample was the PSWM weighting of three hours and a half hours (210 minutes) allocated to the task of producing a social inquiry report (NAPO, 1979. If this was a correct reflection of probation officer activity in writing reports, the time taken to produce reports in this sample would cluster around that time.

The first analysis showed that eleven reports (26%) had taken 210 minutes or less to prepare. The minimum time taken to prepare a report was two hours (120 minutes). However fourteen reports (33%) were recorded as taking more than five hours. It was thought relevant to have a more detailed breakdown of the timings, to try and give a more accurate reflection. In the first instance the total time logged by report writers had been rounded to the nearest ten minutes, but in re-coding each report over five hours reports was rounded to the nearest five minutes. Table 5.2 below indicates the range of times which were recorded for all reports. The time taken ranged from two hours (120 minutes) to ten hours (600 minutes).

Table 5.2
Time taken to prepare reports (total sample)

Less than the PSWM		More than the PSWM	
Time	No.of reports	Time	No. of reports
120 mins	1	220 mins	5
130 mins	0	230 mins	1
140 mins	0	240 mins	1
150 mins	0	250 mins	2
160 mins	0	260 mins	1
170 mins	1	270 mins	4
180 mins	0	300 mins	2
190 mins	5	310 mins	4
200 mins	1	340 mins	2
210 mins	3	360 mins	1
		390 mins	2
Total	11	415 mins	1
		435 mins	1
		450 mins	2
		465 mins	1
		480 mins	1
		600 mins	1
		Total	32

(The spread of times logged is wide, therefore not all times are recorded. If no reports were logged against a time it is not recorded.)

Table 5.2 demonstrates that the majority of reports took more than the time calculated as the average time by the PSWM, although eight reports took less than the PSWM average. The Home Office have always argued that there should be an averaging out of the time spent on any one task. In this sample the average time taken to prepare a report was 4 hours 45 minutes.

The greatest cluster of reports, twenty three (53%), took between 190 minutes and 270 minutes to prepare. However eighteen reports (42%) took over 270 minutes to prepare. It has been argued consistently that the exact time is not the focus of this research. The collection of the information about timings, and the need to round up the figures confirm that hair trigger precision is neither possible, nor appropriate. However it is argued that the circumstances in which the timings were captured in this project reflect more accurately the time that it takes for officers to prepare reports when attempting to achieve best professional standards. An important aim of this project was to identify what factors influence the time taken to prepare reports.

Who takes the most time?

The average time for officers in Team A (the court team) to produce a report was four hours and forty minutes (280 minutes), while it took the officers with generic workloads, Team B, an average of five hours nine minutes (390 minutes).

Team A's sample included the report which took the shortest time to prepare reports (120 minutes). There was a cluster of five reports (17% of the total Team A sample) which took 190 minutes to prepare, and ten reports (34% of the total Team A sample) were completed in 210 minutes or less. However, the sample from Team A included the report which took the longest time to prepare (600 minutes). In addition to this report, which involved special circumstances, seven reports (24% of the total Team A sample) took more than five hours to complete.

In comparison Team B (the generic team) had only one report which took 210 minutes to prepare, and no reports were completed in less than this time. This team had a similar number of reports (seven) reports which took over five hours to complete. This constituted 50% of the total Team B sample.

It is apparent that officers in the court team generally took less time to complete a report than officers with a generic workload. This may be because officers in the court team are more confident at writing reports. They may also be more familiar and adept at consulting other professionals and relevant documentation, or it may be that systems are in place for specialist court teams which aid the writing of reports.

Factors influencing the time taken

In addition to the skills and practices of the officers writing the reports, there are other factors which might influence the time taken to prepare reports.

It might be assumed, for example, that one factor influencing the length of time it takes to prepare a social inquiry report is the level of difficulty. It is not always possible to discern the level of difficulty in any one report. It may be to do with issues which are raised within the interview with the defendant which are not necessarily recognised by any formal method of recording activity related to the production of social inquiry reports. There are, however, some assumptions about level of difficulty which can be tested out.

Destination of the report

It is possible that the court for which the report is prepared might influence the time taken in that crown court reports are generally on offenders who have committed more serious offences, or who are thought to be in need of a more severe sentence.

Nine of the reports prepared for magistrates court (29% of all reports for the magistrates court) took 210 minutes or less and they included the report that took the shortest time. Only two reports for the crown court took 210 minutes or less, and crown court reports included the report that took the longest time.

The average time for the preparation of reports for magistrates court was 268 minutes, while the average time for preparation of reports for crown court was 343 minutes. This suggests that more time was taken over the preparation of reports for the Crown Court. One related factor is that magistrates court reports had to prepared within a tight time schedule, while the offender was on remand. For both of the teams involved in the research the remand period was three weeks. Crown court reports are usually prepared in a longer time scale because a number of factors pertaining to court business, and the demands of preparing complex legal cases mean a delay between committal to crown court and the hearing. In both teams crown court reports were prepared pre-sentence on offenders who were pleading guilty.

Highest previous disposal

One indicator of the difficulty of a report is the criminal career of the offender, which is often reflected in the sentences which had been given for previous offences, the previous disposal. Offenders who had been previously sentenced up the tariff, that is had received suspended sentences or custodial sentences for previous offences, might demand more time because they were at risk of being given a custodial sentence. This was particularly relevant at the time of the research, which pre-dates the changes brought about by the 1991 Criminal Justice Act. At the time of the research, offenders' previous convictions and previous sentences were taken into consideration when being sentenced for a current offence.

There were ten reports (23% of the total sample) prepared on offenders who had previously had sentences of imprisonment. Of these reports none were completed in 210 minutes or less, and five took the longest periods of time - ranging from 415 minutes to ten hours (600 minutes).

In fourteen reports (32.5% of the total sample) the highest previous disposal was recorded as not relevant, which means that there were no previous convictions. This sub-sample included the shortest report written in the shortest time (120 minutes). The longest time it took to write a report where there were no previous convictions was 6 hours 30 minutes (390 minutes).

The majority of reports, nine, in this sub-sample took 220 minutes or less to complete and were therefore very close to the time allocated by the PSWM. However, the average time to write a report on a defendant who had no previous convictions was 223 minutes. This suggests that previous disposal did influence preparation time in that reports on offenders without previous convictions, on average, took less time. This may be because there was less documentation, such as previous probation records, to be consulted.

Sentence

Another indicator of the degree of difficulty in preparing an SIR might be the sentence that was passed on the defendant for the offence committed. It could be assumed that reports on defendants sentenced to imprisonment are the most difficult to write, and therefore take the longest time, while reports on those who were subsequently discharged might be assumed to be more straightforward.

Discharge In this sample the greatest number of sentences that were passed were discharges. In eleven reports (26%) the defendants were given a conditional discharge. In this sub-sample of eleven, four reports had taken 210 minutes or less to prepare and the longest time that it took to prepare a report was 310 minutes. The average time for the preparation of a report which led to a discharge was 237 minutes.

Probation The next most common sentence was a probation order. Eight reports (19% of the total sample) were prepared on defendants who were subsequently placed on probation. Of these, none was completed in 210 minutes or less. The timings recorded for the preparation of reports on defendants who were placed on probation ranged between 220 and 465 minutes, with a cluster of four reports which took between 340 minutes and 390 minutes to prepare. The average time that it took to prepare a report on a defendant who was placed on probation was 342 minutes.

Community service The sub-sample of reports on defendants who were sentenced to community service orders (CSO) also numbered eight reports. Because of the liaison necessary to make a recommendation for CSO it could be assumed that these would, on average, take longer to prepare. It has to be remembered that the timings did not include the time spent with members of CSO teams for the purposes of assessment. It was therefore significant that the shortest time recorded for the preparation of a report in this sub-sample was 190 minutes, and there were four reports which took this length of time. The longest time it took to prepare a report on someone who was ultimately sentenced to CSO was 415 minutes, with the average time being 236 minutes. It may be that, because officers were aware that the court was considering a sentence of community service, they referred the defendant immediately for assessment, rather than undertake lengthy assessment interviews themselves. This finding reflects the limitation of simple workload measurement calculations based on worker activity, rather than tracking cases through agencies, in the face of work practices which increasingly involve collaboration between workers. The total input into the SIRs on defendants who were sentenced to CSO, should of course include the work undertaken by all those employed by the probation service.

Imprisonment The next largest sub-sample was a group of six reports (14% of the total sample) which were prepared on defendants who were sentenced to periods of imprisonment. These included the report that took the longest time to ten hours (600 minutes). The shortest time that it took to prepare a report on a defendant sentenced to imprisonment was 200 minutes. This report, on a defendant with no previous convictions charged with driving with excess alcohol, did not contain a recommendation for imprisonment. The average time recorded for the preparation of reports on defendants subsequently imprisoned was 378 minutes.

The findings appears to support the suggestion that reports which are more difficult, if a sentence reflects difficulty, take longer to prepare. However, as the comments in the section on community service reflect, it may be more realistic to look at the recommendations in the reports prepared to see if these reflect levels of difficulty and demanded more preparation time.

Recommendations

Prior to the 1991 Criminal Justice Act probation officers traditionally made recommendations about which disposal might be most effective in preventing re-offending, or dealing with the factors which had contributed to offending behaviour. Such a practice has, in recent years, been the subject of discussion, but generally probation officers were expected to comment on the offenders likely response to supervision, if a probation order or community service order was made by the courts. In the period that the research was being undertaken specific guidelines produced (Home Office 92/1986) encouraged officers to review all sentencing options available and feasible, making specific recommendations only where that is felt to be appropriate. This 'sentencing options' approach was not universally adopted, and at times contradicted local policies (Godson and McConnell, 1989). The reports prepared by officers in this research in general carried a specific recommendation.

Discharge In analyzing the recommendations in the reports the largest sub-sample was the set of reports which recommended a discharge. This involved twelve reports (30% of the total sample) and the average time recorded for the preparation was 164 minutes.

Probation The next largest sub-sample consisted of eleven reports (26% of the total sample) which recommended probation, with the average time for their preparation recorded as 347 minutes.

Community service Interestingly, those reports which recommended CSO took a much shorter time to prepare, the average time recorded as 212 minutes. As indicated above in the section on sentences, where an assessment for CSO has been made the task has been performed by workers in the CSO service and not by the report writer. Therefore, although the report writer might spend less time on the report, the amount of service time on the report might be quite considerable.

Imprisonment Only two reports recommended imprisonment. One of these took just 210 minute to complete and the second, for a defendant convicted of rape, took 340 minutes. This latter timing might suggest that it is be the seriousness of the offence which cause probation officers to spend time preparing social inquiry reports.

The two reports which took the longest time to prepare, ten hours (600 minutes) included a report prepared on a male with a significant number of previous convictions charged with an offence of robbery. The report writer noted in his self evaluation that he followed the practice of offering sentencing options because he found himself in a 'considerable dilemma' because of a strong commitment to the benefits that probation intervention could provide, but acknowledging that the offence was likely to attract a custodial sentence. The defendant was subsequently sentenced to a period of imprisonment.

71

The report which took the next longest time to prepare (480 minutes) was on a defendant who was convicted of indecent exposure, and the report contained no clear recommendation. The length of time here reflected the complexity of the offence which meant making a recommendation was problematic. However, the fact that a defendant had had so much time from a professional worker, and the court did not ultimately receive an informed opinion from that worker, has implications for the management of workloads, and the involvement of professionals in the process of making assessments.

Offences

The comments in the preceding paragraph indicate that a further measure of difficulty might be the seriousness of the offence committed. As with many of these indicators, it is not always possible to assess seriousness from the descriptions in the documentation. There can be no question of the seriousness of an offence of rape, but offences of theft can range from minor sums to large scale thefts. It is not surprising therefore that the largest sub-sample of reports, nine reports, were prepared on defendants who had been convicted of offences of theft. The average time recorded for preparing reports on defendants who have been convicted of offences of theft was 214 minutes.

The spread of reports against other offences means that the numbers of reports prepared for each offence category are so small that analysis is not helpful. An overall picture indicates that the shortest period (120 minutes) recorded for the preparation of an SIR report was for an offence of fraud, and the longest preparation time was for a report on a defendant convicted of robbery (600 minutes).

Having said that, other reports which took over five hours to complete included reports on defendants charged with offences of indecent exposure, rape, possession of class 'A' drugs and burglary, but also included offences of shoplifting and minor thefts. While in general it would appear that the more serious the offence the more time the report took to prepare, there are obviously other factors which can influence the time taken to prepare reports. From the above analysis, one of the most significant factors which influence the time taken in preparation is the place of the defendant in the 'tariff' system. The implications of this are those defendants who have a considerable criminal career, or have committed offences which may attract a custodial sentence, receive more of the probation officer's time in the preparation of reports. In terms of targeting professional resources, and the probation service's commitment to diverting offenders from custody this is an appropriate use of probation officers' expertise.

Effectiveness

If the probation service is devoting significant amounts of time to the preparation of reports, and those reports are to be used by sentencers to make appropriate decision which have maximum impact of the offender, and take into consideration the protection of the public, then it is important to assess whether the documents produced are effective. As indicated in the previous chapter, in the absence of feedback from sentencers, four measures of effectiveness were devised: take up of recommendations; officer satisfaction; defendant evaluation and independent evaluation.

Take up of recommendations

In this sample the take up of recommendations was 70%. This means that in thirty of the reports written the sentence of the court was the same as that recommended by the probation officer writing the report.

The greatest discrepancy between recommendation and sentence was in the use of community service by the courts. It was used as a sentence in three out of the four cases where it was recommended by the probation officer. In the fourth case a discharge was given instead of a community service order. However, community service was also used in five cases where the probation officer had not recommended it. In two of these, the probation officer had recommended a fine, and in a further three the recommendation had been for discharge. Therefore, in this sample, the majority of community service orders were made where there had been no recommendation by the probation officer, and therefore no assessment by the probation service about suitability for community service. This is significant when sentencers are using a disposal which depends on the professional assessment of the probation officer.

The other set of recommendations where there may be discrepancy between sentencers and probation officers is in the use of the probation order. In all eight cases where a probation order was made it had been recommended by the probation officer writing the report. However, in a further three cases where probation had been recommended the defendants were sent to prison. This discrepancy is particularly significant in a climate where the probation service was targeting offenders at risk of custody, in an attempt to divert them from custodial sentences, by recommending supervision in the community, which would reduce the risk of further offending.

Officer satisfaction

The questionnaire used to record the time and activity involved in preparing the reports also asked officers to record their own satisfaction with the individual report. Where there was dissatisfaction they were asked to comment on the causes.

In twenty five (58%) reports officers expressed satisfaction with the completed report, while in sixteen (37%) officers expressed dissatisfaction. In a further two reports this section was not answered. Of those officers who expressed dissatisfaction in relation to specific reports, twelve gave reasons.

Table 5.3
Causes of officer dissatisfaction

Reasons given	Number of responses
Number of interviews held	3
Not being able to attend Court	2
The written report	2
The data collected for the report	1
Multiple reasons	3

These responses related to the activities involved in preparing the report. Officers were also invited to comment on what had contributed to the cause of the dissatisfaction. In ten of the responses listed in the table below time is a factor, either directly of indirectly.

Table 5.4
Contributory factors to the feeling of dissatisfaction

Factors	Number of responses
Pressure of other work	8
Lack of time	1
Lack of co-operation by the defendant	1
Multiple contributory causes	1

It is difficult to correlate levels of satisfaction to length of time taken to prepare the report. While the officer preparing the shortest report expressed dissatisfaction with it, the officer taking the longest time to complete a report did not record a response in this section.

Consumer satisfaction

Seventeen defendants (39.5% of the total sample) who had been the subjects of reports returned the consumer questionnaire. Of these, eleven

74

said the reports were either helpful or very helpful, and only three respondents found the reports unhelpful. A further three respondents thought they were neither helpful or unhelpful. No respondent thought that the reports were very unhelpful.

The reasons for unhelpfulness included:

Because he didn't tell the Court anything they didn't know from my own admissions.

I stressed to my solicitor and probation officer that I would have preferred a steep fine instead of community service as I am self employed and work most Saturdays. The point was not emphasised too strongly.
(Defendant sentenced to Community Service.)

With such a small sample, relating helpfulness to timings does not tell a great deal. For example, of the three reports that were thought to be unhelpful, one took 210 minutes to prepare, another 270 minutes and a third 415 minutes to prepare. The recipient of the greatest amount of officer time in preparing an SIR found it a very helpful process - even though he was sent to prison.

All the comments relating to helpfulness of reports concentrated on the information that the report gave about the person and how this influenced the Court. Only one person acknowledged any direct effect on sentencing:

I could have been sentenced to a prison term but because of the report I was put on probation, a great relief.

This seems a realistic comment as the defendant had preconvictions and was being sentenced for charges of inflicting grievous bodily harm and theft.

An analysis of the satisfaction of officers in relation to the assessment of helpfulness of the reports by the defendants reveals that in four of the reports described as very helpful by the defendants the officer was satisfied. In one report in this category the officer was dissatisfied, and in one there was no response recorded from the officer. In the three reports described as unhelpful officers expressed satisfaction with two of the reports, and dissatisfied with the third.

A further measure of consumer satisfaction is whether further information was requested of the probation officer. This measure acknowledges that there is more than one consumer of an SIR, and in most cases it is more accurate to describe sentencers and others involved in the criminal justice process as consumers, while the defendants are the subjects of the reports. If a report does not provide appropriate information, sentencers and others might require the probation officer to provide additional information, either by being present in court and being questioned about the report, or by preparing a written addendum to the court. It is also possible for defendants to ask questions of probation officers in court. All of these options add to the workload of preparing an SIR, but they do enhance the service given to the courts, and defendants.

Further information was requested in only six cases (14%), although in three cases it is not recorded whether or not further information was requested. In only two cases did the defendant request more information, and in both of these the report had taken about five hours to write. In fact, all except one report where more information was requested took over five hours to write. One report, where a solicitor requested further information, took 220 minutes to prepare.

On this small sample it is not possible to draw firm conclusions, but it may be that requests for more information are related to complex situations and/or contain controversial recommendations. For example, in one case where everyone - the court, the solicitor and the defendant - wanted more information, the offence was indecent exposure and the recommendation depended upon the medical report which was not available before the court hearing. This report was recorded as having taken eight hours (480 minutes) to prepare.

A further factor influencing the request for more information might be the presence of the probation officer in court. If an officer is presenting the report, there may be more inclination to ask questions, but if special arrangements have to be made to call the officer to court this might act as a disincentive.

Independent assessment

As it was not possible to access directly the views of sentencers on the reports, a means of analyzing was devised in order to produce an independent assessment. By using a points score system it was intended to reduce the amount of subjectivity. For example, one report was assessed by the points score as 'good' on the basis of the content but was thought by the reader to be written in a lax style. However there is no evidence that the use of split infinitives influence the courts sentencing behaviour.

On the basis of the assessment exercise only one report was found to be unsatisfactory - and this report had taken 435 minutes to prepare. Twenty three reports (53.5%) were classified as excellent, seventeen as good and two as satisfactory. Only two of the reports classified as excellent took 210 minutes or less to prepare, while eight of the reports classified as good took 210 minutes or less to prepare. Fifteen of the excellent reports took 270 minutes or more to prepare.

The average time to produce a report classified as excellent was 315 minutes, which would seem to suggest that reports which met all the requirements of the Home office guidelines, and could therefore be deemed to represent best professional practice did take considerably longer than the average documented in the PSWM. Significantly the 'excellent' referred to information contained in the report, which would have been acquired as a result of interviewing defendants, and significant others. This finding therefore relates to the activities which officers undertook in the preparation of reports.

Activities involved in the preparation of SIRs

In analyzing the questionnaires completed by officers against the expectations of the circular, it was assumed that there would be eight major categories of activity:

- Interviewing the defendant
- Home visiting the defendant
- Interviewing other members of the defendant's family
- Contacting other professionals
- Reading related documents
- Writing the report
- Consulting with Senior or colleagues
- Attending Court

In attempting to understand the complexity of workload measurement it is possible that relating these activities to recorded timings and to the overall time taken to prepare reports provides some indication of the activity and workload involved in preparing a social inquiry report.

Interviews with defendants

While the Home Office document does not prescribe the number of contacts required with the defendant during the preparation of a social inquiry report, it is identified good practice to see the defendant at least twice; to obtain information, verify it and share the conclusions with the defendant.

In this sample twenty one defendants (49%) were seen only once. These included five reports where the defendant was in custody. It is not surprising that the latter were seen only once because remand prisons are frequently at some distance from probation offices, and at the time of the research there were constraints on the use of private transport for professional activities.

Of the remaining reports, seventeen defendants were seen twice and five on three occasions times. There seems to be little correlation between numbers of contacts and time taken to prepare the report. The longest report was prepared on a defendant in custody who received only one visit. Of the reports that were completed in 210 minutes or less, eight involved only one interview (including one defendant in custody); two involved two interviews and one had three interviews.

Home visits

A surprising finding in this survey was that in only two reports was a home visit undertaken. While there is no specific instruction in the Home Office Circular (92/1986) to undertake home visits, the requirement to check the accuracy of important pieces of information (8.iii. p.6) and to set the defendant in her or his social and domestic circumstances (10. p.7) suggest that home visits would be required in many, if not all, reports.

The two reports in which the officer recorded home visits took 210 minutes and 600 minutes. While it is dangerous to speculate on such a small sample, it is apparent that involvement in visits to the home might add to the time taken to prepare reports. This is also significant because officers who expressed dissatisfaction with their reports identified lack of contact as one of the causes of their dissatisfaction. Those officers who identified lack of time as a cause of dissatisfaction might have felt constrained in the number of interviews or home visits undertaken.

Interviewing other members of defendant's family

Although home visits were not necessarily undertaken, there was contact with members of the defendant's family, usually in interviews conducted with the defendant. In six reports partners were interviewed and in two reports parents were interviewed. In one case the victim of the offence was interviewed. These interviews took place either with the defendant present, or close to the interview with the defendant and separate times were not recorded for these contacts.

Contacting other professionals

In thirteen reports (30% of the total sample) no contact was recorded with other professionals. Of the thirty reports in which there was contact with other professionals the contact recorded is presented in Table 5.5 below.

Table 5.5
Contact with other professionals

Professional	Number of contacts recorded
Other probation officer	14
Solicitor	11

DHSS prosecutions	2
Hostel staff	2
Magistrates Clerks	1
Crown Prosecution Service	1
Naval Personal and Family Services	1
General Practitioners	1
Psychiatrist	1
Electricity Board	1
Police	1
Local Authority Social Worker	1
Psychotherapist	1

The total recorded here is greater than the sample because for some reports more than one person was contacted. Also, the contact with other probation officers includes those referrals to community service schemes. In six of the eleven reports completed in 210 minutes or less other professionals were contacted and this was usually another probation officer. While in only eight of the remaining reports, which took more than 210 minutes to complete, there were no contacts with any other professionals. Contact with others outside the probation service therefore can contribute to the time it takes to complete a report.

Consulting related documents

Consultation for the purposes of writing reports also involves consulting documentary sources. These can include previous probation records, court depositions and other sources. In twenty reports (46.5% of the total sample), there was no reference to consulting any other documents. In the remaining reports, documents consulted included those listed in table 5.6 below.

Table 5.6
Documentary sources consulted

Sources consulted	Number of consultations recorded
Previous probation records	6
Previous SIR	4
Crown Court depositions	4
Doctor's report	1
Psychiatrist's report	1

Crown Prosecution summary   1
Case conference minutes   1

In only four of the reports which took over 210 minutes to complete were no documents consulted. Therefore it seems evident that consulting documentary sources contributed to the time taken to prepare the report.

Writing the report

This is perhaps one of the most contentious measurement in the process of preparing reports. Officers were asked to log the time they took to write the report. It is acknowledged that the process of writing a report is probably a continuous one, which begins at the point that the report is allocated to the officer. Certainly the thinking and reflecting which takes place during the period of remand for each report, and during which information is being collected and collated, will contribute to the final document. However, it is assumed that the responses to this section reflects the time taken to actually produce the written document.

Producing the written document obviously created demands on officers' time, often paralleling the amount of time spent in contact with the defendant.

Table 5.7
Time taken to produce written document

Time taken	Number of reports
Less than 60 minutes	2
60 - 90 minutes	19
95 - 120 minutes	8
125 - 150 minutes	3
155 - 180 minutes	6
Over 180 minutes	5

Not surprisingly both reports which were written in less than an hour were among those which took 210 minutes or less for the whole process of report preparation. The longest time spent on writing a report which was completed in 210 minutes or less, was two hours (1 report). However the reports which took the longest writing time, i.e. over three hours, did not necessarily contribute to the longest total preparation time. For example, the two reports which took the longest preparation time overall were written in less than three hours.

The Home Office circular (92/1986) does not give guidelines on the length of a completed social enquiry report, but a document of two pages was thought to be appropriate in many probation offices. In this sample, reports from both the teams were of similar layout, typeface and paper size. Thirty reports were between one and two pages long. The maximum length for a report was three pages (3 reports). There does seem to be a correlation between length of report and length of writing time, with four of the five reports which took over three hours to write also being over two pages in length. The thirteen reports which took less than two hours to write were all between one and one and a half pages in length.

Because of this relationship it is not surprising that the shorter documents did seem to take less time in terms of total preparation time. All eleven reports which were completed in 210 minutes or less were two pages or less in length.

Consulting with senior or colleagues

There are a variety of practices relating to consultation about social inquiry reports. Some offices have a procedure where at a certain time in the week any officer can discuss reports they are preparing and, in particular, the recommendation. This process of gatekeeping has now been extended by NAPO who recommend that reports should also be monitored for stereotypical assumptions, mainly on the basis of race and gender, which might lead to discriminatory recommendations. These policies will have significance for the time that it takes for the total preparation of social inquiry reports.

In this sample twenty two reports were discussed either with a senior probation officer or a colleague. Those that were discussed ranged across all the total timings. However, in the eleven reports that took 210 minutes or less to prepare, only three were discussed with another person. Of the twenty one reports which were not discussed with anyone, twelve were completed in 220 minutes or less. This indicates that, in most cases, consultation did add to the total time taken to complete the report

Court attendance

Another contentious issue for probation officers in the total process of preparing reports is whether they should attend court when their reports are presented. In this sample only fourteen reports had probation officers in court when they were presented and this obviously added to the time taken to prepare the report. In the preparation of only one report which took 210 minutes or less, the probation officer attended court.

Conclusion

This chapter has presented the results of the research which involved probation officers logging the activities connected with producing reports for the courts, according to best professional standards. In analyzing the results it becomes clear that a number of factors affect the time taken to prepare reports. Officers who were in the specialist court team took less time than those with generic workloads. Also, reports written for crown court tended to take longer than those prepared for magistrates court. The level of difficulty of the report, if this is based either on the offending history of the offender or the sentence received, also affects the time taken.

The chapter also documents the various activities involved in producing court reports, and it is evident that time spent in face to face contact with offenders is only a small part of the preparation of reports, with the actual writing of the document presenting a considerable workload. The implications of these results, and how the process of capturing the information contributes to the overall discussions about workload measurement systems will be dealt with in the next chapter.

6 Workloads: measurement and management

Introduction

The conclusions that can be drawn from the results given in the previous chapter need to be set in a number of contexts. The first is that changes in activities involved in preparing court reports reflect emerging practice guidelines and policy expectations and will influence workloads. Second, the analysis of these activities have implications for discussions about the changing role of the probation service in the criminal justice system, and specifically the relevance of a qualified professional opinion in the sentencing patterns of the court. Finally, changing patterns of welfare provision or, more accurately, the managing of this provision, have major implications for the use of workload measurement systems.

The original research was designed to question the allocation of actual time measurements to the task of writing court reports, arguing that systems to date had not allowed opportunities to capture timings which reflected best professional practice. In doing this, the process of attempting to capture the workload of a social worker in precision timings was to be explored and analyzed. However, as the results were emerging, the territory was already changing. Initiatives in the organization of social work agencies, reflecting a growing managerialism, were already well advanced. Such initiatives depend upon some notion of workload measurement, of accounting of the work undertaken by those providing the services, which ultimately contributes to decisions about the cost of services.

Debates that focus on the cost of services cannot be separated from consideration of quality of service offered. Quality is inflenced by the time allocated to perform the task. It is unlikely in an era of public spending cuts that workers will be allowed the luxury of specifying their own workloads, or the time they need to perform them, because differential abilities and practices of workers might lead to inequalities in the distribution of work which might not reflect efficiency measures. However, quality of service must be part of the agenda in a culture of consumer rights and charters, and it is necessary for those performing the tasks to argue for measurements which include a recognition of quality. An optimum measurement of the time taken to perform a 'good enough' service might be all that can be negotiated. This chapter will reflect on the results of the specific research project and will discuss the implications for front line workers and managers. This will serve as an introduction to the wider debate, which will be the subject of the next chapter.

Workload weighting implications

Timings

The first, and perhaps most obvious, conclusion that can be drawn from the results presented in the previous chapter, is that it does take probation officers on average longer than the 210 minutes which was the workload allocation for the preparation of a social inquiry report at the time of undertaking the research, derived from the PSWM. The average time taken to prepare a court report in this survey was 4 hours and 45 minutes (285) minutes which was over an hour longer than the previous documented average time.

While it would be attractive to argue that this difference in time recorded related to the method of capturing the activity involved in preparing court reports, it is possible that other factors were operating. One explanation is that it actually did take longer to prepare reports. The process of preparing a social inquiry report changes over time and the expectations of, for example, Home Office circulars or the greater complexity of sentencing options has added to the task of preparing social inquiry reports, which may influence the time taken. Additionally, targeting more serious offenders may have contributed to increases in time taken. The argument that the overall number of reports prepared has reduced, therefore officers take longer (May, 1992) is a more complicated assertion, suggesting the maxim that work expands to fill the time available. It makes no reference to the possibility that the quality of the reports might be enhanced by the increased input of professional time.

However, what can also be deduced from the results of this project is that, even when asked to prepare social reports for the purposes of the research, probation officers were not following all the requirements set out. If they had, then the times logged may have been even longer.

The most unexpected finding is that probation officers did not undertake home visits for the purposes of collecting information for the preparation of reports. While home visits are not always appropriate (where an offender is homeless or living in a bed/sitting room for example), it is unlikely that the majority of this sample came from defendants in these circumstances. Home visits are extremely time consuming, not least because they involve travel time. The PSWM allowed for the inclusion of travelling time as a separate calculation but it is apparent that a home visit would involve further contact with the defendant, which in itself would add to the time taken to produce the actual document. The relevance of home visits to quality of report can be questioned. Significantly, the expectation to undertake a home visit for the purpose of writing a PSR under the 1991 Criminal Justice Act is not made explicit in National Standards (Home Office, 1992). For the purposes of relating quality to workloads, these guidelines are unclear, 'it is the professional duty of the report writer to assess what is the correct amount of detail to be investigated and included in a PSR. More detail than is necessary should be avoided **as being wasteful of time and resources**'(emphasis added) (Home Office, 1992, p12). While the suggestion that a practical judgement should operate, drawing on professional skill and experience is reassuring in one sense, it is not helpful when trying to establish a baseline activity for the purpose of workload measurement. The only required activity (Home Office, 1992, para.15 p15) is that the offender should be interviewed, although there is an acknowledgement that to obtain the necessary information may require more than one interview. However, the lack of clarity in national standards is not helpful when probation officers in the survey reported lack of time as a problem, even when encouraged to spend as much time as necessary on a particular task. This is not to suggest that officers should be held to account to perform specific tasks, but they should be able to invoke best practice guidelines when undertaking a piece of work and negotiate an appropriate time scale. Such a position became significant with the introduction of the 1991 Criminal Justice Act, which recommended short remand periods for the purposes of writing court reports. An enquiry into the requirement that pre-sentence reports should be prepared more quickly (such reports were known as 'expedited' reports, CPO 33/1993), found that the standard of those 'expedited' PSRs prepared for crown courts was low, especially those prepared in one day (Home Office, 1994). The conclusion of this enquiry however, is that 'probation services must improve the quality of PSRs' (1994, p14), not that more time should be given to the preparation. It is apparent that national standards have not been introduced to protect staff workloads, but to set up expectations of staff activity, against which they will be assessed, irrespective of the resources available.

The results also indicate that in higher tariff cases, that is those defendants who have already had considerable criminal careers or have committed offences which warrant a sentence which might involve loss of liberty, probation officers do spend a great deal of time preparing social inquiry reports. During the period in which the research was undertaken, and indeed since, there has been a significant debate about the role of the probation service in the criminal justice system. There have been concerted efforts to encourage and enable probation officers to focus their work on high tariff offenders through a policy of diversion from custody. The first stage of PSR writing, as outlined in National Standards, is 'evaluating seriousness' (Home Office, 1992). Also, it is at the point of writing social inquiry reports that intervention can be most effective in the process of diversion. Additionally, focused work such as the use of Offender Gravity Rating scores, Risk of Custody scales and Targeting Matrix (Hampshire, 1994) have drawn attention to the need to present arguments which might influence sentencers and offer opportunities for rehabilitative sentences. That the task of writing a social inquiry will become more significant in the sentencing process is reflected in the requirement of 1991 Criminal Justice Act for reports which make proposals, rather than recommendations. While greater focus and the use of predictive tables may well assist the probation officer, it is likely that writing reports on higher tariff offenders will increase the time it takes to complete the report.

The argument put forward by the Home Office when negotiating the PSWM weightings was that some tasks will take longer than others, but that in the monthly calculations of officers' work these will average out. However, if the baseline measurement is not accurate, then the average weightings will not reflect the workload. This is apparent from the average weighting which emerged from the analysis of this research into the workload associated with preparing court reports. More particularly, if workloads are to include writing reports on offenders at greater risk of custody, then the average weighting will increase. This will have particular significance for probation officers performing specialist functions, such as court team officers whose workload comprises writing reports.

Activity

Linking good practice to time taken is also significant when considering the quality of written reports. While many reports in the sample were deemed of good quality, only one explicitly followed the 'sentencing options' approach recommended in the Home Office circular (92/1986), which was the guidance available at the time. This report took significantly longer, but this was for a number of reasons only one of which was the time taken to explore the options in the written report. A requirement to undertake such an activity will lengthen the time spent on the actual writing of reports.

Another example of good quality practice, or more particularly quality assurance, is the practice of gatekeeping. This has accompanied the focus on high tariff offences outlined above, and is the process by which reports prepared by one officer are read by a colleague. Initially the focus was on recommendations for sentence, and the scheme was designed to monitor whether officers were recommending inappropriately high tariff offences, rather than offering a variety of measures within the community which would address the identified causal factors for the offending behaviour. In the late 1980s the process of gatekeeping was expanded to cover monitoring for anti-discriminatory and anti-oppressive practice. The aim of gatekeeping was then to ensure that content, style and recommendations reflected equal opportunities policies of the probation services and, by doing so, to improve the quality of the service provided to offenders and to ensure that the requirements of section 95 of the Criminal Justice Act 1991 were met.

Arrangements for gatekeeping differ between services, and not all operate such a system. One team in the sample had such a policy, which was organised by means of a weekly team meeting to consider recommendations. Other services carry out the process by means of an individualised pairing system, and each report is read by the partner officer. Whatever the gatekeeping arrangement, it requires extra time spent by the officer in presenting the report to the team, or discussing it with a colleague. It also therefore adds to the total resource commitment to the preparation of the report, in that the time of the second officer needs to be acknowledged in an overall calculation. Such quality control mechanisms are of crucial importance in the preparation of reports in the view of sentencers and researchers. Processes which are designed to improve the quality of the service will add to the total time spent on the task of preparing the report, but ironically will mean more time spent in activities which do not involve contact with the defendant.

While not specifying the practice of gatekeeping, National Standards issued following the implementation of the 1991 Criminal Justice Act do specify the need for quality control in preparing PSRs (Home Office, 1992, para.35 p22). Significantly, in the list of possible activities, some of which would impinge upon the time taken to prepare reports, no mention is made of ensuring that enough time is allocated to each report, or that the number of reports to be prepared at any one time should be rationed. Indeed, the suggestion that one indicator of quality is the urgency with which certain reports should be prepared is directly counter to an expectation that quality reports take time to prepare. The concluding sections of the National Standards are concerned solely with the ways in which 'probation officers will do all that they can to try to ensure that proceedings are not delayed unnecessarily' (Home Office, 1992, p29). Hence probation officers may have to short circuit quality in order to expedite proceedings (Home Office, 1994).

The debate over of the use of probation officer time in activities other than client contact will be further exacerbated by the changes brought about by the organisation and delivery of services from partner agencies from the independent and voluntary sector (*Partnership in Dealing with Offenders in the Community*, 1992). These changes, which require probation officer to liaise with others in order to produce packages of punishment in the community, will add to the tasks required of officers writing court reports and therefore add to the total preparation time. The partnership document had been preceded by the Green Paper *Supervision and Punishment in the Community: A framework for action* (Home Office, 1990b) which indicated that 'probation officers' traditional casework skills will have to be supplemented by skills in orchestrating services provided by others' (para.9.2 p30). The implications for report writing are that a number of people will have to be consulted when making proposals to the court because, 'delivery of the programmes can involve a great many people apart from the probation service' (Home Office, 1990b, para.9.5, p30). As has been said, this commissioning of traditional probation officer activities to other organisation has led to real concerns about the future of probation officers. However, some reassurance is gleaned from the observation that at least some professional skills will be required for the preparation of court reports (Home Office, 1990b, para.9.6, p31).

The significance of activities involved in preparing a PSR are reinforced further in yet another consultative document. *Strengthening Punishment in the Community* (1995) confirms the need for PSRs to be prepared by the probation service, but questions the roles and activities involved in the task. In the debates about the changing role of the probation service, which accompany this consultation, findings about the effectiveness of intervention become increasingly significant.

Writing reports

A significant finding reported in the previous chapter is the amount of time spent writing the report. The evidence which indicates that this constitutes a major part of the workload raises concerns for probation officers and ministers alike, in that routine clerical and administrative tasks should not be undertaken by professionally qualified social workers. This constitutes a misuse of skills and a waste of a trained workforce in the eyes of ministers, and is frustrating for workers because it detracts from the face to face work with offenders. However, it is difficult to breakdown time spent on actually writing the report between the clerical tasks and the professional. If, as National Standards states, sentencers will require 'interpretation and analysis of factual information collected ... and coherent and logical argument in support of conclusions' (Home Office, 1992 para. 26, p18) this clearly requires the time of a professionally qualified worker who has the knowledge base and the appropriate skills to undertake the analysis. It is the thought and consultation which goes into this process, not the mechanics of producing a written document which is time consuming.

A further factor which will influence time taken to write the actual document is the focus on high tariff offenders. It is apparent from the results of the research project that the greatest amount of time spent by probation officers is in administrative and clerical tasks, not face to face contact with defendants. Reports on high tariff offenders will require more time spent consulting depositions, verifying information, liaising with others and, probably most significantly, writing the report. The impact of reports in cases where the liberty of the individual is at risk, and the impact on victims needs to be considered, will obviously require careful consideration and therefore more time.

What is measured

The above discussion also highlights some of the imprecision in analysis when attempting to measure workload. As well as not being able to separate out task from process it is also difficult to capture all the activities. This is discussed specifically in relation to assessing the appropriateness of a community service order (CSO). Each defendant considered for CSO had an input from at least one other worker in the probation service, but these timings are not captured in this study. The significance of this finding in the changing context of report writing is that if an offender is to be referred to a variety of projects run by organisations other than the probation service, more time will have to be spent liaising with such organisation and making referrals. National Standards for the preparation of PSRs under the 1991 Act acknowledge that specialist advice or assessment may be required (Home Office, 1992, para.20, p17), that a referral mechanism might have to be established at the PSR stage and that that stage might also be an appropriate point for the detailed planning for supervision. The results documented in the previous chapter indicate that all additional activity, liaison and consultation add to the workload, and therefore the time taken. Further requirements for consultation will undoubtedly contribute to additional time and effort being spent on the preparation of PSRs.

The identification of the need to capture all work involved in a particular activity or process is significant in discussions about researching workloads and the place of workload measurement in decisions about allocation of resources to the probation service. The question which needs to be addressed is whether the measurement is of work undertaken by individual officers, or is of all work undertaken by the service in respect of an individual case. This issue has been explored in this study in relation to referrals for CS and to the activities involved in gatekeeping, but it relates to other aspects of the work of the probation service. Offenders who are subject to orders which require day centre or group attendance will have a variety of inputs from workers who are not the supervising officer. While the data required has implications for the way that the research project is set up, it has particular significance for the purposes to which the results are put. If the results are to be used to protect the work of individual officers, to monitor their performance, then systems to log all their activity are required. If the results are to be used to negotiate resources, then all the work involved in each particular order or report, should be logged.

The concept of capturing time taken raises issues about both recording and measurement practices. The NARS study was criticised because logging activities every fifteen minutes was seen to be unrealistic, with officers working hard to demonstrate that every fifteen minute period was crammed with activity. The study described in this text could be criticised because it depends on the commitment of officers and their rigour in recording times. Bamford, for example, criticises any diary exercise because it can 'record only the worker's own perception of his (sic) activities, not always the most objective of assessment' (1982, p44). It is no less objective than other perceptions. In some professions (significantly the legal profession) where activities carry a charge, logging time per activity is a common practice, used to ensure that the appropriate fee is charged.

The impetus to get accurate time measurement when they are to be directly linked to costs was an important factor in setting up the NPS, as will be discussed later. The attempt to provide a more accurate account of probation workloads led to the NPS devising a third way of capturing the total timing of activities (May, 1992). This involved officers recording actual starting time, and the duration of all activities which lasted ten minutes or more. The conclusions indicated that the time taken to write reports had increased from the NARS survey in 1977 thus supporting the results documented in the previous chapter. Specifically the NPS logged that the time taken to write SIRs on adult offenders for the magistrates court was 240 minutes, and for the crown court, 245 minutes. The differentials were not therefore as great as those in this study, but this might be explained by some tasks (phone calls, for example) not being capture because they took less than ten minutes. Also, despite publicity by NAPO and clear guidelines that all work was to be captured, and that the survey was not a time and motion study, there was no specific instruction to attempt to undertake the task according to the principles of best professional practice.

It has been acknowledged that the original NARS was obsolescent at the time of its introduction in 1979 because new activities were introduced by criminal justice legislation. As has been documented, major policy changes in the preparation of court reports followed the completion of the data collection in the survey described in this text. The timing of the NPS study, which reported in 1992 faced similar challenges, but it is significant that the major impetus was from the Home Office's desire to implement a system which would provide data required for the information systems which would give analysis of activities involved, and resources used in the treatment of offenders, but more particularly, the cost of these resources.

In this context, what is measured is integrally linked to how it is measured, and why it is being measured. While the conclusions of the previous chapter are that it is not possible to capture time measurement of workload with hair trigger precision, and indeed it is not desirable to do so, the introduction of information systems demands accurate workload measures. Bamford's prophecy that 'while the search for clarity of objectives remains valid, less attention is now being paid to workload measures' (Bamford, 1982, p44) is simply untrue. In being more specific about objectives, and who is employed to achieve them, policy makers are requiring even more precise information about workload measurement. The alternative to workload weightings, which reflect accurately the resources used, is the use of continuous time recording. This method of recording workloads has been eschewed by professionals, not least because it has notions of 'clocking on' which are alien to the concept of the autonomous worker. Additionally continuous time recording is unwieldy and, ironically, time consuming.

The specific context of the current initiatives in information and resource management systems and their effect on policy and practice will be discussed in the next chapter. Before moving on to this consideration has to be given to the relevance of the findings on workload measurement for the management of workloads.

Workload management

For those who are engaged in the performance of social work tasks to wait for long term surveys and results is as useful as having a workload measuring system that tells you that you were very busy last month. One conclusion reached in this text is that no matter how precise the measuring system is, it is useless unless it is incorporated into some form of management system. A second conclusion is that workloads can be measured, but by any definition that measurement is bound to be imprecise. Whether precision is important relates to the purpose of measurement, which in turn introduces the notion of workload management.

Allocation

Whatever system of workload measurement is used it is of little benefit to individual or teams of officers if it is used in a vacuum, merely to measure work done. While it may be initially comforting for workers to know that the feeling of overwork and stress is a reality because a measurement of workloads illustrates that they are doing too much, such an analysis demands more than an imprecise conclusion which does not tell the extent of the overworking. It also demands an assessment of what constitutes 'enough' work, so that the work done can be assessed against such a yardstick. Also, any sense of relief will soon begin to pall if the information is used to document the overwork and do nothing about future allocation, or redistribution of existing workloads. Workload management schemes involve a dynamic interaction between information acquired and decisions about resource allocation. This is predicated upon open and accountable systems for capturing workloads, a cooperative relationship between supervisor/manager and individual worker and collaboration between all team members. The overall aim is to estimate, in the light of measurement of existing work, the capacity of workers to take on work. Allocation then takes place according to the expected demands of any individual piece of work and how that equates with the space available in the workers overall workload. One of the major purposes of such schemes, from the perspective of the line manager, is to ensure that work is allocated and that such allocation is perceived as fair and equitable by all those involved.

The basis of this process is that it is anticipatory and not retrospective, but it demands certain preconditions and has far reaching implications for social work, or indeed any work setting. The preconditions are that any system of measurement has to be undertaken consistently, be relatively easy to apply and be able to produce information swiftly.

Management tasks

To introduce and maintain such a system requires specific activities by front line managers. The first of which is to negotiate an agreed measurement system which involves an audit of all the work to be done. While having applicability across the team, or organisation, it should also allow for special circumstances which might prevail at any one time. Such circumstances might relate to the office or organisation, or individual workers. Workload measurements that are acceptable to all participating and take into account a variety of factors which are not to do with assessment based on detailed social work diagnosis and treatment plans are easier to negotiate, and more effective to operate.

The next activity involves introducing systems to enable workers to provide information on work undertaken efficiently and accurately. This has to be accompanied by systems for plotting incoming work and identifying all demands on the individual, team or organisation. While these may well be linked to existing systems for collecting statistical data for other purposes, it is important that specific feedback is given on the information collected and used for the allocation of workloads. Often this will demand making public information pertaining to individuals, but this is necessary to ensure both an understanding of the operation of the system, and an acknowledgement of the different contributions of all workers. In the probation service, the differing demands of, for example, writing reports and supervising high risk offenders need to be debated and acknowledged.

Front line managers have a specific role in working with individual workers to manage specific workloads allocated. This involves identifying priorities, giving permission to undertake certain activities and, conversely, not undertaking other tasks, making decisions about closing cases, referring on or offering a different service. This role differs from that traditionally identified as supervision, but involves strategies for dealing with the work allocated, and as such may involve discussions about resource needs (for example, in terms of secretarial support).

Finally, in terms of specific tasks for the purposes of workload management the front line manager will need to identify, and negotiate with others, both within the organisation and outside, a fall back position for unallocated work. This might include rationing, waiting lists or other systems for controlling the incoming flow of work.

In such a model, workload management operates at a variety of levels, but is designed to ensure 'best possible professional practice is a joint responsibility of both the individual practitioner and her (sic) organization. Practice is sure to founder, and practitioners are sure to become disenchanted or burnt out without both members of the partnership acting responsibly and in concert'(Bottoms and Stelman, 1988, p120). The initial negotiations are at team and individual level, agreeing on the systems of measurement and what is to be measured. The next level has to be a joint activity between line manager and individual worker, but this leads to further management activity within the agency, re-negotiating with other workers and clarifying demand and expectations of others of the team. Finally, there has to be individual worker responsibility for workload management, a degree of self management without the intervention of the manager. If such systems operate effectively, the need for scrutiny and supervision becomes less necessary. Self management allows individual workers the opportunity to make professional decisions about interventions and ways of organising the allocated workload. Individual styles and areas of interest could operate on the understanding that the total workload is 'manageable' within the agreed workload allocation. At one level this appears attractive because it maintains a level of professional autonomy and enables workers to make their own decisions. It does not

93

provide the protection that accountability and joint decision making offers, for example, when one or more cases 'blow' and others have to wait their turn, or get no service at all. Nor does it offer the level of supervision which gives the opportunity to explore possible methods, make sense of difficult and conflicting information or merely offload some of the feelings engendered by the work.

A further limitation is that it does not offer any inspectorial check either at the basic level of ensuring that work is done or, a more qualitative analysis of the standard of the work done. However such quality assurance systems should be part of wider management systems (for example, routine inspection of records), although cannot be entirely separated from the workload allocated. More positively if systems of workload allocation could be streamlined and taken out of the workload of managers then this may allow more time to provide professional supervision to front line workers and operate quality assurance mechanisms.

Management role

It could be argued that such a model is mechanistic and denies the complexity of the management task within social work. To merely operate systems which enable workers to cope with all that is allocated, or expected of them from government policy, denies the role of the professional. However this raises fundamental questions about the autonomy of professional workers, but also about the links between resource allocation and quality assurance. For example, in the results presented in the previous chapter, should the role of the senior probation officer be to ensure that, irrespective of the conditions in which probation officers are preparing reports, home visits should be undertaken on those offenders who have a home? If it is, then how can systems be devised to enable seniors to monitor activities in the preparation of each report. Or more pertinently, how can such systems be established without being unwieldy, bureaucratic, time consuming and undermining of the professionals judgement? In terms of public accountability and guaranteeing a quality service however, it is important that good practice is carried out.

Additionally, if tasks are not being conducted, or not being carried out to an appropriate standard, then this is the responsibility of the front line manager. It may be that, as was reported in this survey and in the Inspection report on crown court reports (Home Office, 1994), officers did not have sufficient time. If this is so, then some re-negotiation of workloads may be necessary, and the need to argue for extra resources becomes paramount. This may be necessary to guarantee the quality of the service but, just as importantly, it may be necessary to protect the worker from the long term effects of stress which ultimately leads to burn out

(Cherniss, 1980). Such protection reflects the responsibility of the manager for staff welfare, but also for the preservation of valuable and costly resources.

This analysis of the role of the front line manager also raises questions about the extent of the intervention of managers in the activities of front line workers. For example, McDonald (1994), in assessing the use of behavioral methods by probation officers, argues for a proactive role for managers who should be asking workers to justify the exclusion of particular methods from their repertoire of skills. This expectation is made on the basis of findings that behavioral methods are more effective than others. However, such a management role takes managerialism one step further than supervision, and risks a scenario where the piper who calls the tune is the individual team manager. While this may be a justifiable position if there was definitive evidence that certain interventions are more effective than others, but it may give licence to front line managers to censure activities which are seen to be less relevant, or challenging to individual values. The experience of female social workers in having to justify women-centred practice to male managers is an example of a potential area of conflict. McDonald's (1994) invective against probation managers, and a commitment to a particular style of effectiveness in social work is no less results-led and part of the notion of management by objective which has been identified as alienating and de-motivating for staff. This tension between the allocation of resources, and the expected results from the investment of resources is at the heart of the implementation of performance indicators and information management systems which are part of the wider context discussed in the next chapter.

Workload rationing

A further aspect of the role of the front line manager referred to above is to use workload measurement schemes to plot the allocation of resources and identify shortfalls. If workload management systems are adopted, and attempts made to give each individual officer the potential to work to her/his maximum efficiency by protecting caseloads, what happens when individual ceilings are reached and, more particularly, what happens when team or office ceilings are reached? Bradley's work (Glastonbury et al, 1987) indicates that the arbitrary nature of ceilings can be counteracted by the individual case review system. This however is time consuming, and does not go far enough. There is no point in measuring workloads unless you are going to use the measures to inform decisions about cut off points, which involves setting ceilings, and operating rationing and priority setting systems.

In the first instance, if a piece of work cannot be allocated to one officer it is allocated to another. But it is essential that the basis of this re-allocation is known, hence the need for a publicly accountable system. In the event of all officers working to capacity (ie. having reached their ceilings) it is important to have agreed strategies in advance. There are a number of possibilities, the most common one being to take on the work and acknowledge that the individual or team is overworked. A second possibility is to trawl all workloads to prioritise cases and make choices between existing cases and new ones, which would lead to discharge of those which were deemed to be lower priority. A third is a 'safety valve system' which operated in Coventry (NAPO, 1986). If officers in one team reach their ceiling work, and significantly for the purposes of the survey discussed in this text, court reports, are diverted to another team in the area. A final, and more radical solution. but one which is gaining increasing support in social work agencies, is to have a cut off point, a workload ceiling. In the Coventry system, for example, if divisional overload was reached, the court was informed that extra time is required to prepare the reports.

There are, of course, ways in which such courses of action can be anticipated. For example, decisions about recommendations in reports can directly affect caseloads; organisation of office duty or court duty can affect workloads. However this depends upon the whole system being open and public, requiring officers to give up some of their autonomy in return for protection of their workloads.

However, acceding that workload ceilings offer worker protection does not mean that such a course of action is wholly positive. There is concern for potential consumers who are not getting a service, and in the case of the probation service this may mean longer periods on remand in custody while waiting for a report to be prepared, or a less effective sentence if the court has proceeded without the benefit of a report. Also the organisational outcomes might not be totally effective. The claim by Davies et al (1988) that workload measurement which proves that an organisation is overworked magically produce resources might not be verified. However, if an organisation constantly works to a ceiling, the argument for extra resources is never made unless the unallocated work is logged systematically and produced as evidence. Alternatively, within a given area, if individuals and groups are consistently refused a service then they will cease to ask for it and the 'need' will have been seen to disappear. Thus the operation of ceilings might not produce extra resources but may lead to a redistribution of existing resources, or policy changes which lead to a negation of the need for the service. Such outcomes are at the heart of the debates about the probation service which are highlighted in the next chapter.

Conclusion

This chapter takes as its starting point the results presented in Chapter 5, identifying that, by the particular methodology used it is possible to demonstrate that probation officers do take longer to write court reports than had previously been acknowledged. However, the purpose of these findings is not to argue for hair trigger precision in the measurement of workloads, but to demonstrate the complexity of the process of capturing all the activities involved in the performance of a particular social work task. In doing this, the chapter begins to highlight the political agenda that surrounds workload measurement,

This agenda is discussed in more detail in the next chapter but, as a precursor to this, and to continue the discussion of the function of workload measurment for the protection of front line workers, there is a discussion about the place of workload measurement in workload management systems, focussing particularly on the roles and responsibilities of the front line manager. Throughout these discussions the tension between the performance of individual workers and the allocation of resources is highlighted.

7 The wider context

Introduction

This chapter acknowledges all that has been documented so far in this text about workload measurement in the probation service, but sets this in the wider context of a changing political agenda. Since the work on challenging the allocation of specific workload allocations began there have been significant policy developments which have implications for the process of measuring workloads or, more accurately, the utilization of the outcomes of measurement exercises. These developments have included efforts to introduce a financial or resource management information into the probation service. In documenting the implementation, the chapter will explore the redefinition of workload management and identify how notions of workload measurement are being used by policy makers, managers and workers for political ends.

At the beginning of this text a retrospective view of the development of, and need for, workload measurement systems was presented. However, the changing climate due to far reaching policy initiatives creates a need to review workload measurement and its role in wider management activity. During the late 1980s all social work agencies were the focus of intense activities around audit and performance indicators. The explicit purpose of these activities was to ensure value for money and accountability for public spending. Underpinning such activities is also a thinly veiled attempt to deprofessionalise social work. Nowhere has this been more apparent than in the renewed interest in workload measurement. To collect data about the performance of tasks within an organisation by workers of different grades prepares the way for developing policies which argue for the performance of tasks by those of a lower, or unqualified grade because this is more economic. This is particularly so if the only data that is being collected is the time it takes to perform the task, with no evaluation of the quality or effectiveness of the work. This chapter uses the critique of workload measurement schemes in the probation service to provide a commentary on the description of the policy initiatives around policy and resource information.

Background

In 1972 the introduction of workload measurement systems in the probation service was acknowledged to be directly related to resource allocation. This was reinforced in the revised weightings in 1979. The National Activity Recording Study (NARS) which informed these revised weightings was quite specifically designed to produce information for a number of purposes, including determining priorities. Although claiming that the agreed weightings were the result of best professional practice, it is apparent from the critique of the methods used to obtain these weightings that they did not necessarily reflect the time necessary for workers to perform tasks to their best professional ability. However, the measures produced did produce a system devised to assist individual probation officers. They were part of nationally agreed code and conditions of service which attempted to identify what output might be expected from a worker in a given time period. Workers in the probation service were successful in achieving some measure of protection by negotiating the use of the agreed workload measurements in workload management. By linking the allocation of time per task with a negotiated ceiling for the number of hours to be worked in any four week period, they also incorporated some measure of improving performance, even if the weightings themselves did not measure effectiveness; 'allocation of time, of course, does not of itself give any measure of effectiveness, but consideration of the actual as opposed to expected use of time may be helpful in improving effectiveness' (NARS, 1978).

This would seem to be an appropriate application of workload measurements and reinforces the view that in workload management, effectiveness is not only about the amount of work that is undertaken by an individual, team, office or service (i.e. the turnover), but also the way in which that work is done. Workload weightings or measurements should therefore enable officers to work to best professional standards with each individual case. As the discussions in Chapter 6 have demonstrated, it is the task of front line managers to use workload measurement in an effective system of work allocation, monitoring and prioritising to protect workers and ensure a quality service for users.

However, since the late 1980s the role of the middle manager in the human services has been usurped by the intervention of policy makers. Workload measurement became part of higher management initiatives which had little to do with the protection of individual workers, but more to do with rationing and commissioning of resources. Audit Commission reports (1986; 1989) and the introduction of financial and resource management information systems meant that workload measurement was becoming part of a complex political agenda. This agenda involved the analysis of social work tasks by cost, which led to a further analysis of whether they needed to be performed, and if so whether they required a professionally qualified social worker to perform them. Tasks could be downgraded so that they might be undertaken by less qualified, or even unqualified staff, who would command lower salaries and might be employed outside statutory/public sector agencies. A worrying consequence for those qualified as social workers was that their professional existence was being questioned.

These initiatives are not confined to the probation service. The National Health Service and Community Care Act 1990, for example, introduced care management as a way of delivering services in the community. This included many skills which are traditionally identified with qualified social workers employed by local authority social service departments. The legislation, however, stated clearly that care managers did not necessarily have to be qualified social workers (Department of Health, 1989; Orme & Glastonbury, 1993). Also, under the auspices of user choice and needs-led services, there was a clear message that the policy of care in the community, was to be care by the community, with the burden of care falling upon families, neighbours and volunteers. There is no doubt that such initiatives were ideologically driven, but it was the ideology of the market which informed these changes, which were to impact directly on the work of professional social workers (Orme & Glastonbury, 1993).

In suggesting that the probation service should be multi-disciplinary, the Audit Commission (1989) first mooted that it should be made possible for services to grant aid independent agencies and local community initiatives where appropriate. The resonance with the community care initiatives is clear. Explicitly, a multi-disciplinary service would employ a range of specialists, and the report recommended that 'the overall management of offenders would be undertaken by the officer holding the order -"the case manager". This officer must ensure that all elements fit together and standards are maintained' (Audit, Commission, 1989, p66). Probation officers would not, under such a model, spend time in direct work with offenders, but would co-ordinate services provided by others employed by a variety of voluntary and independent agencies, who would not necessarily hold a social work qualification.

This organisation of the delivery of service was brought to fruition in the *Partnerships Document* (1992) which gives financial incentives to contract for

100

services with projects in the voluntary and independent sector. Furthermore, although the Home Office consultation document (1995) acknowledged a clear role for probation officers in assessments for the courts, its recommendations for a community order could lead to the probation order ceasing to exist. These recommendations were accompanied by the Home Office *Review of Probation Education and Training* (Dews, 1995) which argued against the requirement that probation officers are required to have a social work qualification in order to be employed by the service. If probation orders do not exist, there is no need for probation officers to supervise them. If there is a sentence of community punishment, then this can be administered by Community Correctional Agents, who do not need social work qualifications.

Information systems

While the changes in the probation service were in part driven by a particular commitment to removing the social work base of the probation service and creating a correctional agency which would complement policies driven by slogans such as 'prison works', the arguments had to be framed in terms of economy, efficiency and effectiveness. The recommendations for the re-organization of the probation service follow a long period of negotiating an information system for the probation service which commenced in 1982 with a Financial Management Initiative to devise a financial management information system (FMIS). The aims of the initiative were: to provide integrated financial, activity and staff information in order to give probation committees and managers within an area, the information needed to support policy planning and related budget development; to monitor performance against area objectives and priorities; to provide information to ensure that resources are utilised an effective, efficient and economical manner; to facilitate the development of delegated budgets; and to enable specific probation service activities to be costed (Home Office 1989a).

The beginning of the process to produce a comprehensive information system for the probation service included the Statement of National Objectives and Priorities (SNOP, 1984) which heralded the introduction of management by objectives (MBO), and a debate about the role and function of the service within the criminal justice system. While SNOP was concerned with the redistribution and more efficient and effective management of resources, it required every service to respond with its own local targets and objectives. The widespread commitment to MBO heralded the need for information systems to monitor what tasks were being undertaken and whether the objectives set were being achieved. This had implications for the use of workload measures.

The management consultants appointed in 1986 to develop FMIS worked alongside representatives from the Home Office and the probation service. While seeking to integrate existing information from the service, the development team acknowledged that a crucial piece of information missing from the analysis of resources was information about time spent on the various activities undertaken by workers in the service. Time was seen as an essential resource and an essential building block of FMIS. From the outset the consultants met objections from probation officers who argued that simple time measures did not adequately reflect the complexity of the work done (Crawforth, 1987). They argued consistently that the aim was not to make value judgements about work carried out, but to identify time and activities. However measurements included outputs such as the number of successful completion of community service orders, or the number of high or low tariff offenders supervised. Implicit in these crude measures are judgements about what tasks the service should be performing and to what extent it was achieving these tasks. The outputs used were based on criminological data and took no account of any objective other than cessation of offending behaviour. The initial system recording information was even more basic than that. As those involved at the time commented, the quality was measured on rates of activity, and 'the question of quality of work done - unless measured by level of contact - remains unanswered and if we include wider social work criteria - our effect on homelessness or unemployment - the picture becomes inevitably more complicated' (Crawforth, 1987 p61).

At an early stage it was recognised that to calculate the cost of an activity, information was needed about how much staff time was being spent each of the activities. Initially a system of time sheet recording was devised to identify tangible outputs and the proportion of a team's time spent on activities relating to those outputs. Management in these situations would involve some trade off in terms of time spent on other activities, or the team would have to be more efficient (i.e. take less time) on the specific activity of writing reports. Here was the first area of contention. In merely measuring the status quo, without any notion of expected workload ceilings, the implication is that if demand increases on a certain activity (e.g. report writing) there will be no proportionate increase in resources. In fact, in financial terms, if staff can undertake more tasks by completing them more quickly this leads to greater economies. Such an accounting system does not include the cost of offenders who re-offend because the reduction of probation service input has led to less effective intervention.

If it did prove possible to increase the resource, information would be used to determine how best those resources could be used to meet objectives (Farenden, 1987). However, by that stage work patterns would have changed and an information system would not capture unallocated work. Also, work which had assumed a lower priority, and was therefore taking less time would be measured as such, without any recognition of the downgrading of the activity.

The second stage was to include time spent on less tangible outputs. Effectiveness was to be measured by assessment of how far objectives had been met, but when discussing resources, quality of service as an objective becomes one of those intangible objectives.

These developments were not universally popular in the service. The FMIS team attempted to alleviate anxiety which focused specifically on the collection of data about the time allocations for officer activity, by acknowledging that there would be local differences. The benefits were underlined in terms of front line management, in that 'even the rather broad allocation of timings that would result from these proposals **would give managers useful information about how resources are being used'** (emphasis added) (Home Office, 1989a), but it did not give reassurance that, if necessary, additional resources would be allocated. The team openly acknowledged that the information about timings would be directly linked to performance indicators. An efficiency scrutiny of the Home Office Probation Inspectorate had been carried out (Grimsey Report, 1987) and was critical of the Inspectorate for having no systematic means of evaluating and comparing the performance of different areas. A firm recommendation was the development of performance indicators and it seemed logical to those involved that an information system could be used to complement the implementation of such indicators.

The response of NAPO to these initiatives emphasised that, without knowledge of which strategies and interventions are effective, and lacking the means to determine this, the original purpose of FMIS becomes reduced to a means of planning and controlling budgets (NAPO,1989a). This concern was reinforced by the draft specifications for FMIS which asserted that 'it is not expected that FMIS will give information about quality of work, but will just focus on the supply of information to help areas judge their progress towards effective achievement of objectives' (Home Office, 1989b para 56, p19). All of which has to be considered in the context of a mission that FMIS is to be 'a catalyst to encourage a process of change' (1989b, para 60, p20) towards a management style which was new, and probably alien, to the probation service. This management style was to include objective and target setting linked to resource targeting, with devolved responsibility for service delivery. More significantly, devolved responsibility meant being responsible for the cost of services.

The FMIS draft specifications, while recognising the sensitivity of time recordings (1989b, paras 67-70), were emphatic about their place and significance in the process of resource targeting. The implication of this emphasis on time recordings and the consequences of integrating different information within an overall system becomes clearer when, in a section on notional times, the report makes specific reference to 'staff utilisation by grade' (Home Office, 1989b, para 113), and acknowledges that hours of work by different grades will be differentially costed. The explicit purpose of FMIS was to translate activity timings into costs, which in turn will allows for comparison between officer grades, teams and areas. The evidence, that some tasks were performed more cheaply by staff on lower grades, would be captured, again without any acknowledgement of the quality or the effectiveness of the performance of the task.

The sensitivity of this change of culture was recognised and a Home Office discussion paper (1990a) suggested that notional times for activities would provide probation areas with the opportunity for 'self-examination work' (1990a, para 13). Here at least was a more positive role for front line managers. However, even this self examination would take place in an information system that 'would make it feasible to carry out analysis of the cost of individual probation activities, and/or the amount of time spent on them' (1990a, para 15). The use of notional timings, i.e. global timings for particular tasks, based on some form of calculation, such as those developed in the 1970s and 1980s and reviewed in this research, were seen as offering a benchmark, which could be applied by the Inspectorate when examining area performance (1989c, para 21). In a sense they were to be used against the service, by introducing invidious comparisons, rather than as a tool to ensure that staff were given protection and clients assured of a high quality, professional service.

It is therefore not surprising that NAPO's response questioned the effectiveness of the information system and its ability to link outputs, costs and effectiveness in a meaningful way. They highlighted the emphasis of FMIS on the quantification of the extent to which policy objectives would be achieved, rather than acknowledging quality (NAPO, 1989). This was supported to some extent by the Audit Commission report on the probation service (1989), which criticised the policy initiatives for their micro attention to value for money, while ignoring the broad argument that community based penalties are less expensive than custodial ones. In particular, the conclusions of the Audit Commission report (1989) that, while there was a need to demonstrate effectiveness and for management systems with clear lines of accountability for the financial arrangements, it was 'unnecessary to develop large complex systems; a better approach is to develop a flexible system tuned to local targets and objectives' (1989, p30). Overall, the Audit Commission was critical of the FMIS especially because it was elaborate, expensive and concentrated on efficiency with little attention to effectiveness. The Commission took a more realistic approach to the relationship between resources and outcomes, in that it suggested that 'the extent to which services contribute to reduced (or at least contained) offending must be related to the resources they consume' (1989, p600). However, it did not abandon the FMIS approach totally in that it concluded that, if services have equal impact on offending, but one uses fewer resources, 'then it is more efficient, and efficiency is just as important as effectiveness' (1989, p60). It further argued that monitoring had to be introduced alongside 'a robust system of performance indicators (which) could make a contribution to enhancing the credibility of the service **as well as assisting internal resource allocation'** (Audit Commission, 1989, p61).

Workload measurement or, in the language of FMIS, notional timings, had an identified place in the construction of an information system, whether it be for financial or resource calculations. This distinction between the need for information and resource calculations is highlighted by the change of name for *Financial* Information System to *Resource* Information System(RMIS), which was thought to be more acceptable to the probation service, and a more accurate description of the scope of the system. However, allowances were still to be converted into a monetary value (RMIS, 1990 section 5, assumption 8), although it was recognised that, it might be more useful if the value was calculated as a 'unit of resource' (RMIS, 1990 section 5, assumption 9). Significantly, in response to NAPO's criticisms, a fourth level output was included which would involve identifying the quality of service as defined by consumers of the service. The inclusion of such an evaluation was thought to make the systems more acceptable to the probation service.

Work measurement would be on an activity basis within each team. The calculations performed by RMIS use the amount of time spent on each activity and the number of occurrences of each activity at team level. Thus the work performed by a particular probation officer, or the work performed on a particular case, would not be recorded as distinct items. Furthermore, during the development of FMIS/RMIS a distinction between actual times and notional times was emphasised. Actual times were seen to be more accurate, flexible and directly relevant; but more costly and complex to collect. Notional times were seen to be easier to use, enable priorities to be allocated and had historical acceptance in the probation service. This was an important distinction, in that the agreed workload weightings were described as 'notional' times, even though NARS had defined them as 'actual' rather than 'expected' (see Appendix). Actual time could only, according to RMIS, be gleaned by continuous time recording by probation officers. While FMIS/RMIS allowed for either system to be used, such a change in definition is significant in that it reflects a continuing quest for hair trigger precision in capturing the resource in-put into activities undertaken by staff of the probation service. Such accuracy is important when considering the cost of service, it was not thought to be necessary when the calculations were merely being used to ensure that probation officers carried realistic workloads.

Linking workload weightings to resource allocation would therefore become quite specific. NAPO's response to the recommendations on the use of workload weighting was negative, describing it as a 'crude system of prioritising' (NAPO, 1991, p3). However, NAPO, was committed to the continuing use of workload measurement to provide some sort of protection for workers. Questions raised about the accuracy of the allocated timings were being coupled with pressure to use the measurement system to impose some form of workload ceiling.

National Probation Survey

The report on stage 3A of FMIS (1989b) led to a second national review of workloads in the probation service, the National Probation Survey (NPS, May,1990). Significantly, the results produced included not only timings for task performed by probation officers, but also information about costs. The results were first used in resource planning in 1991. In acknowledging that workload surveys are of necessity descriptive, not prescriptive, it was suggested that the use of such surveys in resource planning should not assume that the 'current use of resources is the right use of resources' (May, 1992, p2)). As has been said, the NPS attempted to address criticisms made of previous attempts to capture workloads of probation officers and was assisted in this by NAPO who encouraged officers to co-operate, and to log their total workloads, not treat the exercise as a time and motion study. This was done in a spirit of co-operation, primarily because it was envisaged that any revision of existing workload measurements would help address issues raised by the motion which had been passed at the 1989 NAPO Annual General Meeting. More accurate reflection of the demands on probation officers might, at best, lead to more resources including an increase in staffing levels. At worst, they could be used to prioritise and ration work.

However, this was not the outcome for the service. Workloads and workload measurement were becoming inexorably linked to financial management information systems, which in the early 1990s were converted, in name only, to resource information systems. While the NPS was reporting fundamental changes in the work of the probation service were already being brought about by the implementation of the 1991 Criminal Justice Act. As with the earlier review of workloads, the information gathered was rapidly becoming outdated. However, a ominous development in the methodology and results of the NPS was that the work of 'other grades' was included in the survey, significantly that of probation assistants. This paved the way for financial comparisons between the work of qualified probation officers and other, unqualified, staff.

Resistance to such developments was not based on any simple notion of elitism, or the uncritical protection of jobs. While acknowledging the need for accountability for spending public money, NAPO reiterated the need for information about effective practice at individual and group level, suggesting it was as important to probation services as aggregated data about reconviction rates. They argued that if nothing is known about what influences offenders to stop offending, then data about how much it costs is meaningless (NAPO, 1991). Other criticisms of the RMIS proposals to link notional timings from the NPS with financial data were that it involved an over-emphasis on statistical data; there were limitations in collecting data in aggregate form and risks of (mis)interpreting the data. The costs (both financial and resource) of implementing information systems were identified as running counter to the first 'golden rule of performance measurement' that 'the cost of performance measurement must be justified by its worth in relation to informing decision-making and to improving your client's business" (NAPO, 1991).

However, NAPO's stance was not shared by all in the service. Whitehead, from the perspective of an Information Officer, was somewhat more sanguine about management information systems. He argues that the weakness of the probation service was that it had assumed that the vast majority of probation officers were hard working and assiduous in helping and supporting offenders, that is doing a 'good job', without any evidence (Whitehead, 1990). His experience of developing an information system in one area illustrated that 'this local service is now in a better position to account for, and demonstrate effectively what probation officers are doing, and what they are achieving' (1990, p31). Acknowledging that the introduction of management information systems is linked to a change of culture within the Home Office which makes it clear that the only objective for the probation service is the reduction of crime, Whitehead rather naively suggests that the service itself would not have to accept such a goal, but could 'put more emphasis on helping clients with those problems which are amenable to amelioration, and which have been identified by clients themselves' (Whitehead, 1990, p33). While such aims are laudable and a reduction of problems might actually result in crime reduction (Raynor, 1988), it is unlikely, in the criminal justice system of the 1990s, that 'helping clients improve their quality of life' would be an acceptable performance objective. More relevantly, Whitehead confirms that information systems inform managers about work being done, but 'say very little concerning how the work is being done, nor do they explicitly touch on notions of quality. This distinction between the 'what' and the 'how' should be explored in more detail' (Whitehead, 1990, p35).

Whitehead's example of SIR monitoring for the purposes of information systems is a useful one for the purposes of this text. Monitoring of reports focuses on the number of reports written, their recommendations and the sentence imposed. This did not give information about the nature of the relationship between the probation officer and the offender (Whitehead, 1990). While such information might be of little value to managers when deciding about allocation of resources, it would be meaningful in an evaluation of the effectiveness of the service given. A more serious criticism is that such monitoring gave little information about the process of producing the report e.g. whether national standards were adhered to, and what factors contribute to the effective production of an SIR.

To recommend an increase in the level of data collected for an information system might seem invidious, arguing for even tighter managerial control of the actions of probation officers. It might also serve to capture the enormity and complexity of the task of writing a professional assessment in the context of the criminal justice system, which provides useful information and enables sentencers to make appropriate decisions. Such information can, of course, be available by other means. The 'how' might be more effectively explored in supervision by a manager (Whitehead, 1990), but this raises questions about the role of quantitative information, especially that relating to workloads, in the overall management of the service, and in many ways highlights the distinctions between management by objectives and total quality management. The latter acknowledges that, if the conditions in which workers perform their tasks are appropriate, then the standards of the work, the effectiveness, improves. Here is the nub of the debate about workload measurement. Is it merely a quantitative description of the work that is done, according to an arbitrary measure, is it a precise instrument which can dictate resource allocation, including appropriate activities of workers, or is it a means of giving workers protection and thereby ensuring the quality of service?

Information systems and information technology

The debate about RMIS has been dealt with in some detail, because it highlights important issues about the collection of information about workloads. In plotting the resistance, the aim was to highlight the difference of perception between those who wanted to time workloads for the purposes of front line management, to ensure the quality of the service offered and those who were concerned with the amount of work done and the cost of that work.

RMIS ultimately foundered not on ideological grounds, but on grounds of usefulness. Senior managers identified that the outputs were of limited value to them, but recognised that they may be of some value to the Home Office. A more powerful lobby, however, was those, predominantly Research and Information Officers, who had operational responsibility for collecting information. In recognising that information technology had a significant role to play in the service, they argued that 'computer information was seen exclusively about assessing efficiency and effectiveness with little apparent relevance to actual delivery of services to clients' (Colombi, 1994, p81).

The probation service had had computerised information systems for some time, with Probis (Probation Information System) being available from 1983 to analyze data from statistical returns and produce standard workload printouts. It was not resistance to information technology which meant that RMIS was greeted with some cynicism, it was the nature of the system, and the fact that it did not reflect operational needs of the service. In 1992 an Information Systems Strategy Unit was established to deal with the newly emerging client, and other, information systems.

Even though these developments were welcomed as being 'bottom up' it is clear that information to manage workloads was still fundamental to information systems. When an information audit carried out in 1993 found that operational information was weak and contained duplication, inaccuracies, poor integrity of data and data redundancy, there was concern because this impacted on management information making it difficult to 'assess productive time, relative costs of probation work and where improvements might be made. There is little information to enable probation effectiveness to be measured, (IS Study Report and IS Strategy Statement, 1993, p9).

However, in making a distinction between 'work management' and 'case management' the *IS Strategy Catalogue of Applications for Areas* began to articulate how an appropriately resourced and constructed information systems could provide an effective service for the organisation. Work management was described as being about managing resources, e.g. the allocation of officers to cases, case management about maintaining records of individual cases. The interface of the case management system with the work management system provided correlations between case status and effort spent, which underlines the inter-relationship of the different sets of data. Collecting information about quality of input, as well as effort (e.g. number of contacts made) is also important to achieve the objective of the work management application 'to make the most effective use of staff and to ensure work is completed to the required timetable and properly accounted for' (IS Strategy Catalogue of Applications for Area, 1993 p21).

The outcome of IS Strategy was the development of Case Record And Management System (CRAMS) which will contain, among other data, the client diary file relating to the contact with the probation service and the PSR/Report file which will contain diary information relating to reports. It is envisaged that the system will, for example, be able to record the allocation of a PSR to a member of staff and it will streamline some of the routine tasks by, for example, the production of standard letters, access to data about past offences and response to supervision. Such uses of information technology is intended to enhance probation officer activities and the quality of their work, by enabling them to access more information more easily, and in doing so will speed it up, or ensure that certain tasks will take less time (General Application Requirements for CRAMS).

However the introduction of CRAMS is only part of a National Probation

Service Information Systems Strategy (NPSISS) which will ultimately provide a comprehensive picture of information needs, and attempt to meet them. Hence information contained on various datasets including Staff/resources file (to include details of staff workload/availability), and budgets file, which will carry sessional supervisor costs, will be interfaced. Programs which generate statistics from the Client Record file, Client Register file or the Staff/resources file will provide the capacity to correlate worker activity with information required for internal use/management. The benefits of the introduction of information technology cannot be denied, and their direct applicability to effective workload systems was acknowledged at an early stage (Glastonbury et al, 1987). Also, information systems which have been developed with the collaboration of workers, and users, have been demonstrated as contributing to the efficiency and effectiveness of an organisation (Avison & Wood-Harper, 1992).

However, the limitations of the systems, in that they can only be as accurate as the information loaded into them, and the threat that they can lead to correlations between sets of information which may not otherwise be possible, are still cause for concern, even if the worst aspects of RMIS have been avoided. Such concerns are not unique to the probation service; 'in organisations that move towards the use of systems based on the needs of a centralised bureaucracy, once information standards are set debates tend to revolve around issues pertaining to the reliability of that information rather than whether the events represented by those measures are depicted appropriately' (Oldfield, 1994, p188). Nowhere is this more so than in the area of workload measurement.

Workloads and industrial action

The use of notional timings in information systems for the probation service, and the ensuing debate, highlights the political agenda which surrounds any attempt to measure workloads. The criticism of the data collected and used to measure performance was that the measurements were too crude in that they failed to take into account the quality of the service which was being delivered within a particular time scale. They did not measure effectiveness. Such criticisms tended to come from NAPO acting in its role as a professional association and fulfilling its responsibility to ensure a quality service for clients and users. It also recognised that to ensure a professional base for the service, workers had to be able to make appropriate decisions about interventions, drawing upon a knowledge base which included criminology and social work interventions. Appropriate assessment of people who experience social deprivation and who may be involved in addictive behaviour or suffering mental health problems require skilled judgement and time to gather and evaluate all relevant information. The arguments put by NAPO were not therefore a knee jerk reaction to Home Office proposals. NAPO had a long history of collaboration with the Home Office over matters of central resource planning, had instituted the original workload measurement system and had co-operated actively in the two national workload surveys.

NAPO is also the trade union of the probation service, and as such it had another role to fulfil. This involved protecting workers by negotiating appropriate codes and conditions of service, ensuring proper resource levels and protecting jobs. Much of the response of NAPO as a trade union was related to its commitment to a properly resourced probation service within the criminal justice system and was based on the sound professional criteria outlined above. The action that NAPO could take as a trade union was more specific. Dissatisfaction of members with the workload weightings operating since NARS came to a head in the mid-1980s. Workload limitation was first mooted in 1986, when officers were encouraged to work within their contractual hours. This would involve using workload weightings to measure allocated workloads. When the ceiling of 150 hours in a four week period was reached there could be a refusal to accept any more work. Such radical suggestions were not totally acceptable to workers at that time, and the reaction was to call for a revision of the weightings. The resistance to working to ceilings was a reflection of the professional concerns of the service which acknowledged that such action might be in conflict with 'the requirements of clients and their own consciences' (Killeen, 1986). It was argued that before probation officers stopped accepting work there were workload management systems which could be operated. Such systems could include reducing services which were offered e.g. limiting the time that officers were available for duty; not providing support for offenders until they were released for prison or negotiating with courts about appropriate remands for court reports. Other systems devised involved accepting all work allocated but operating a 'safety valve system' (Killeen, 1986), which meant that when a particular office reached its workload target figure (in this case, for preparing SIRs) any subsequent referrals were allocated to other teams in the division. When the division reached overload, then negotiations took place with magistrates for longer remands. In this system workload weightings were accepted as the only measure available, however crude and it was argued that 'schemes based on national workloads allowances could be used locally to reduce excessive working hours' (Killeen, 1986 p6).

The need for workload limitation did not diminish but, in the view of NAPO, in a climate in which the service was experiencing financial cuts, without any comparable cuts in workload, the case for them became even stronger. Invoking the benefits of the workload measurement system, and accepting that the NPS weightings are 'roughly applicable for the majority of the service' (NAPO, 1995, p4), the Trade Union Organisation (TUO) Committee offered a do-it-yourself guide to self preservation, arguing that

111

intolerable workloads cause ill health and undermine professional standards and working practices (NAPO, 1995).

Workload weightings were therefore used in arguments put by both sides of the negotiating table. Managers need them to monitor performance, workers need them to protect themselves and their professional practice.

Conclusion

This chapter has placed workload measurement in a wider management context. In documenting events since the completion of the research outlined in Chapters 4 and 5, it has argued that workload weightings have been used to political ends by both employers and workers in the probation service. The attempts to introduce a financial management information system (FMIS) for the probation service have been described and attention has been drawn to the inexorable link between effective use of resources, cost and workload measurement systems. Acknowledging that 'the largest single cost in any Probation Service is staff time' (Home Office, 1989), an FMIS was to link staff time activity and cost. The chapter documents how the need for more accurate notional timings led to the second national study of workloads in the probation service, the National Probation Survey (NPS). It is argued that there was a direct link between updating of weightings and the requirements of what ultimately became called a Resource Management Information System (RMIS).

The introduction of cumbersome information systems was ultimately abandoned in favour of Case Recording And Management System. These combined the benefits of information technology with the need to collect and analyze data about probation officer activity. The political agenda was to identify the actual cost of the intervention of a professionally qualified probation officer into the lives of offenders. This, coupled with the inclusion of the work of unqualified probation assistants in the NPS and the constant scrutiny of the probation service on measures of effectiveness, prepared for questions about the necessity for professionally qualified social workers undertaking the tasks of a probation officer. This questioning was taken further with the review of qualifying education and training undertaken in 1994. It is argued that such initiatives are intended to deprofessionalise the probation service and prepare the ground for tasks to be contracted out to less qualified workers in the voluntary and independent sector. While diversity of service provision is welcomed, this should be introduced for reasons of quality and not economy.

Finally, in highlighting the wider context of workload measurement, the political implications of workload measurement are further illustrated by NAPO's encouragement to members to use the workload weightings to limit their workloads to the ceilings negotiated with employers.

Conclusion

In the previous chapter (p108) three questions were posed about the purpose of workload measurement: is it a quantitative description of the work that is done; is it a precise instrument which can dictate resource allocation, including appropriate activities of workers; or is it a means of giving workers protection, and thereby ensuring quality of service? This review of the process of devising workload measurement systems for the probation service has illustrated that for many who rely on such systems, or utilise them to a greater or lesser extent in their management practice, they can be all of these things; or none of them.

In suggesting that the times logged in its survey were actual rather than expected, NARS (1979) was claiming a degree of accuracy which this text refutes. By critically evaluating NARS, and cataloguing the difficulties of undertaking research in the area of workloads it is suggested that the factors that influence the process of capturing workload times are so complex that hair trigger precision in the timings collated are not possible.

What are the implications of this conclusion? Should the practice of managing workloads be abandoned? This is not the argument of the text. In reviewing the themes explored, this chapter will also evaluate the significance of the very process that has been taking place. This process has involved attempting to capture the activities of probation officers in undertaking a particular social work task in order to challenge both the time allocations which were previously agreed and the methods by which those allocations had been calculated. In order to do this it was necessary to engage with practitioners on a research project which was focusing, not

113

just on the work that they do, but on the quality of that work.

In describing the particular piece of research attention has been drawn to the resistance of social work practitioners to research, and the results of research. Two decades ago Goldberg and Fruin argued, in the context of researching workloads, that 'the slender body of validated knowledge and social work education in general has not been able to keep pace with these widening and changing demands made on social workers so as to equip them to carry out these varied and enlarged functions' (1976, p8). The relationship between practice and academia is still a source of tension especially in the area researching workloads. Although designed to contribute to a body of knowledge which might influence practice and therefore equip social workers to carry out their tasks and functions, researching workloads can be seen to be part of a managerialist discourse which merely seeks to construct artificial categories and create unrealistic expectations of social work practitioners.

The validation of knowledge and its role in legitimising certain kinds of activity also presents specific problems for social work in the academy which in turn leads to a questioning of the validity of the academic project. Funded research into the criminal justice system is often framed by the ideology of 'just desserts', and outcomes which are counter to the current or favoured ideology can be ignored. Similarly, research commissioned from agencies is often required to enable staff, be they managers or practitioners, to function more effectively within a given system. Such research is not required to question or challenge the system, merely operationalise it. Even if research results are noted and used to influence practice, whether that be intervention with clients, or management practice, this immediately privileges that particular knowledge construction, and this can cause concern among social worker practitioners.

Tension between academics and practitioners is not unusual. In social work they should be reduced by the partnerships which have been developed round the provision of basic social work education (CCETSW, 1991). These arrangements require social work educators to work alongside service providers to ensure the quality of education and training. Such partnerships are not always smooth, and the nature of the relationship has to be subject to continuous negotiation (Ford et al, 1994). In addition, partnerships for the provision of social work education raise questions about which set of principles, beliefs and practices should be privileged in the educational process. Discussions around teaching the principles and practices of care management illustrate the tension. Should the views of practitioner managers, which are framed as a direct result of policy initiatives, override the critical evaluation provided by academics, who do not have to implement the policy, or be held to specific performance indicators? Similar questions have been raised about the changes which have been brought about in social work practice by the emphasis in basic professional education on anti-racist and anti-

114

discriminatory practice (Orme, 1995). It is an irony that, within these debates, the probation service had negotiated the strongest statement of requirements for the education base for the training of probation officers.

The balance between practice considerations and critical commentary is particularly relevant to academic research which investigates what social workers do, how long they take to do it and the implications for quality, of work and of work experience. The experiences of the probation service outlined in Chapter 7, where this evaluation became intricately linked with a specific political agenda highlight how research processes, or the results of research can be subverted. The history of researching workloads documented in this text, therefore, demonstrates why social workers have a resistance to the research process, and distrust the results.

However, the creation of a research base is integral to the development of an academic discipline and a set of professional practices. The conduct of the research and the application of its results can contribute to, and influence practice. As Goldberg and Fruin comment, the lack of definition of the social work task 'does not excuse social workers from becoming more explicit about the problems they are trying to tackle, with or on behalf of their clients, the specific goals they set themselves and the expertise and resources required to explain these objectives' (1976, p7). Practice based research is therefore important both in justifying the interventions of the practitioners, and in arguing for a professional education and training for those who are to carry out those interventions. The need to argue for the academic base of social work is crucial in the light of the review of social work education and training for the probation service (Dews, 1995). The challenges to the probation service are paralleled within social services where care managers are not required to have a social work qualification.

The need therefore is for research which acknowledges the expertise and resources required to carry out effective social work intervention. Hence the particular research project described, in setting out to measure time, documented the complexity of the task of preparing an assessment on offenders who were appearing before the courts. In plotting both the activities and factors which influences those activities, it was able to illustrate that the exercise of logging time was not a simple one, and that policy and resources changes had a major effect on the functioning of practitioners.

The impact of such research is influenced by the perspective of particular stakeholders. For NAPO the purpose of being involved in research on workloads was to provide information to influence the future design of national surveys undertaken by the government. In doing this it can challenge the hypothesis, and the outcomes. For the government, or the employers, the review of staff time management, was an attempt to devise a scheme which facilitated the effective use of resources. The research task was to evaluate the practices and processes involved in the development of systems, and to make observations which would provide information and influence the design of any future survey.

There is an argument that any research is positive because it provides feedback on performance. Social work organisations need feedback in order to change and develop practices (Ross & Bilson, 1989). Feedback can be obtained from seeing the impact of decisions/actions when working with clients, and from academic research. However, the needs of practice and the research undertaken do not always coincide; 'what is missing is information about patterns of response in the local system and ongoing information about the changes in these patterns as policy and practice change over time. Most academic research is not designed to perform these tasks' (Ross & Bilson, 1989, p123). Some academic research does contribute to policy development, but often it is constrained to taking a snapshot at one particular point in an organisation, and this snapshot is at best two dimensional. There are therefore risks, as detailed in the previous chapter, that the information received, the knowledge created and the feedback given can then be used by particular groups to their own ends. Furthermore, as Chapters 2 and 3 illustrate, research into practice rarely provides immediately useful answers for practitioners, so their motivation to participate is weakened.

These are the concerns of the researcher, but they are also the concerns of practitioners who become the subjects (or objects) of research. This has implications for who undertakes the research, who commissions research and how it is disseminated. It also has implications for the way that research is undertaken, both the methodology and the methods. Ross & Bilson, for example, argue that 'the use of research to provide feedback also challenges the idea of research as an independent and objective activity' (1989, p124). This has two consequences for the acceptance of any research, but has particular implications for research into workloads.

First, feedback leads to the generation of patterns which are a way of conceptualising and understanding the interactions of the system, which enables planning to be developed in an orderly fashion rather than through chance, opportunism, political expediency or methodological fads. The patterns presented in research are attempts to produce meaning from information and are crucial for change. However, breaking down tasks for information systems, searching for accurate measurements or instant results leads to greater managerial control, with less managerial accountability or innovation. Research then becomes part of a regulatory discourse. By investigating an activity, that activity becomes privileged, if not legitimised.

The dangers of this process for the research outlined in this text are obvious. Workloads have been caught up in the modernist managerialism of social work accountability (Parton, 1994). This involves the collection of statistics and data which do not relate to the quality of practice and alienate the practitioner, making him or her resistant to the activity both of measuring workloads, and participating in research. The discourse of information systems is integral to the debate about the nature of the management activity within the probation service needed to support the effective operation of such systems. The emphasis in information systems on accountability and standards is seen by some to be counter to the notion of the autonomous practitioner (McWilliams, 1990), although it is also argued that negative implications of management models are less a result of inherent problems of the management structure and more a consequence of the way management roles are exercised (Shepherd, 1990). How do those in positions of authority, with control over, and responsibility for, resources manage these tensions? How do they ensure standards and accountability, while being accountable themselves, sometimes to pay masters who do not share the same ideals? This echoes the notion of pipers and tunes which is a recurring theme in management of public sector organisations; 'we are not and cannot be free agents and the best that any manager (or leader) can do is (a) to seek to influence the formulation and content of policy and (b) to implement given policy so far as is possible in ways which enhance and do not compromise service values' (Shepherd, 1990, p178). Research into workloads which aims to identify resources needed for effective service delivery can be part of that search for influence, and an attempt to uphold service values.

The second set of issues is the suggestion that for the researcher to give feedback, to be involved in the organisation, challenges the objectivity of the process. To make such a criticism suggests that other methods of conducting research are more objective. Random control testing and large data sets which provide complex statistical analysis give a different set of information, they are not necessarily any more objective. More significantly, they are probably less comprehensive, and therefore less relevant to practitioners. Stanley's account (1990) of the role of researchers in social services departments illustrates how much of the data gathered in the research process highlights the manner in which official accounts, based on monitoring and statistical information, tell little about the work that is being done, and renders the workers invisible. This, she suggests, is because researchers are constrained to connect human relationships to numerical research. In undertaking this exercise they often fail to discover all the information, and as such produce findings of limited value. Her case study method demonstrates how social work activity can be documented, analyzed and evaluated for the purposes of feedback which can inform and create change. That the case study was of her own family meant it challenged the orthodox understanding of objectivity. However, it amply demonstrates the feminist claim that the personal is the political, that one person's experience is as valid a piece of knowledge as the sum total of the experience of many. For social work this claim is echoed in Ungerson's work on the documented experiences of individuals who are involved in caring roles and relationships of the most intimate nature. Her

117

title *Policy is Personal* (1987) reflects, not only that each individual's experience is valid, but also that global policy decisions impact on these individuals in different ways. This is equally so for the experiences of workers when systems which are designed to translate their experiences into numbers, whether that be units of time, or some other unit of measurement are set up and researched.

If qualitative methods are employed to attempt to capture data on the activities of social workers, or in the case of the research described here, probation officers, this can highlight the complexity of the interaction between offender and the actors and agents within the criminal justice system, and can serve to demonstrate that the reductionist approach to a skills or competence based analysis of the probation task is not only counter-productive, but is a highly dangerous strategy.

Having reviewed the arguments for the research base to social work practice and organisation it is important to review the outcomes of the particular research undertaken. Significantly, in the light of the documented criticisms of workload measurement systems, it is necessary to question whether they should be maintained within management systems in social work. If they cannot offer degrees of accuracy, if they are part of a management initiative which is challenging the professional base of social work and if researching them merely becomes part of a regulatory managerial discourse, should they be abandoned?

That is not the conclusion of this text. Workload measurement systems have a vital role in social work, not only as part of management systems which seek to be accountable for public spending, but also as part of employment practices which seek protect workers and ensure quality of service to users. More particularly, workload measurement systems have a significant role to play in the current policy initiatives which are producing a purchaser/provider split within service provision.

The introduction of care management has demonstrated the need for appropriate measurement systems. If work is to be contracted out to provider agencies in the voluntary and independent sector it has to be properly costed, before providers can tender and contracts issued. A workload audit is necessary to ensure that all the tasks are captured, and that they are appropriately costed. This is true for organisations who will provide care for vulnerable people in the community, but it is perhaps more significant for providers who have responsibility for supervising those who present some risk to the community, that is criminal justice organisations. The debates about the lack of appropriate levels of resources for mentally disordered offenders highlight this. As well as offering protection by ensuring appropriate resource levels are included in the contracts, proper accounting might challenge the policy on the grounds of economy. It is possible that if the true cost of supervision is known, then the market forces will suggest that supervision remains with the probation service.

In undertaking an audit the tasks that remain with the purchasing agency need to be acknowledged. In reviewing arrangements for assessment for packages of care in care management Stevens (1994) found that there were two major workload implications. One, it was difficult to predict the complexity of the cases which were to be assessed, and therefore the demands they made in terms of time. Two, with no workload scheme, which gave a realistic reflection of demand, the sheer numbers of assessments made it difficult. The consequence of both processes was that workloads became unmanageable, leading to delays and crisis in other work. As Chapter 1 documented, there are a variety of ways to measure workloads, but even with its imprecision, the time per task allocation utilised in the probation service does seem to give the most effective means of predicting potential demands, as long as the time weightings reflect the full extent of the task, and all its component parts. For the probation service the care management assessment is paralleled by the Home Office suggestions for the role of the PSR in community sentencing (1995). If the PSR 'may include an indication of the expected level of supervision, together with some elements of the content of any order that is proposed' (Home Office, 1995 para 3.14, p8) then, as has been demonstrated by the findings of the research documented in this text, the duties of the probation officer will be complex, and the production of the document time consuming. This will be particularly relevant if the PSR is to assist the court in coming to an appropriate decision.

This latter point relates to another powerful reason for having a comprehensive workload measurement scheme which reflects the true demand on provider agencies. For the probation service, the plethora of national standards which are being produced by both the Home Office (1992) or NAPO (1995b), reflect a concern in the era of citizen's charters to ensure quality of service delivery. As NAPO argues, 'quality is not delivering more with less, taking on higher and higher caseloads to protect dwindling budgets' nor is it 'the fastest preparation of reports' (NAPO, 1995b, sect 2). Appropriately devise workload measurement systems ensuring that resources are made available to provide appropriate service to sentencers, quality intervention with clients and protection to the public has to be the aim of all involved in the criminal justice system.

The evidence from the research conducted in this text is that the quality of the work provided by the probation service for the courts has been high, despite demands and constraints made upon the officers who prepared reports. By their own self evaluation the officers identified how systems could be improved to enhance the quality of reports. Also, by critically evaluating the complexity of the task of preparing court reports, and the factors which influence the process, it is possible to argue that, despite its imprecision, the current workload system, as long it is subject to review, and is not interpreted as an absolute, precise measure of the time taken to perform tasks, does at least give a yardstick which will lead to realistic costing which will influence resource allocation.

Finally, the power of the use of workload measurement in industrial disputes has been recognised. However in a climate of performance related pay, and expectations of higher output and greater effort the need for a measurement system to help achieve parity is paramount. Again the aim of measurement is not to try and account for every minute of the working day, or to create a culture of work to rule, but to ensure that some form of negotiation takes place to facilitate the allocation of workloads within the realms of what is feasible and, just as importantly, to ensure that demands are made of staff in a fair and equitable way according to agreed criteria and measurement so that, if performance is to be measured, there is some baseline agreement of what has been expected.

Finally, in coming to these conclusions it is possible to argue that the contribution that properly conducted research makes to social work is that it can empower those who participants in the research. This is as true for the workers in the service as it is for research about the experiences of users of the service. If the conclusion of this text is that workload measurement has something positive to contribute to workload management, it is also suggested that this will only be so if there is a constant review of both the practice of social work, and the measurement process.

Appendix

PROBATION WORKLOAD MEASURE - REVISED VERSION

(approved by the steering committee on workloads in the Probation & After Care Service - April 1979)

In preparing this revised workload measure, the Steering Committee took account both of the results of the National Activity recording Study and of good professional practice. The new measure has been considered and approved by the Conference of Chief Probation Officers and the National Association of Probation Officers.

Like the one published in 1974, this revised measure is applicable only to the work of maingrade officers doing generalist tasks. Weightings are in terms of hours; the fixed allowances are per calendar month. The detailed report (not included in this Appendix) explains how adjustments can be made to allow for differences in the number of working days per month.

The revised workload measure has six components, four similar in type to those in the 1974 measure and two new ones. The six components are:

#1.   Time allowance for each end-of-month case and each report completed. Details are set out on the attached sheet. Weightings now cover all recording and report writing.

*2.   Travelling allowance - 1 hour for 25 miles travel.

3. A fixed overheads allowance - 18 hours per month. This covers kindred social work, the giving of lectures, the supervision of ancillaries and volunteers, attendance at meetings and general "back-up".

*4. Breaks allowance - 18 hours per month.

#5. Student supervision allowance - 12 hours per month. This applies to students on placement for 2 or more days a week. Students on 1 day a week placement - 4 hours per month.

6. Personal special allowance (PSA). This is to take account of such work as court duty, community service work, local liaison and any other tasks which can appropriately be covered in this way. The PSA allowance should be locally agreed on a per month basis and reconsidered at least twice a year.

* - same concept and weighting as 1974 workload measure.
\# - same concept, some change in weightings.

SUGGESTED REVISIONS OF NAPO WEIGHTINGS - PROVISIONALLY AGREED LIST

Supervisory work:	Present NAPO weighting[1]	NARS finding (rounded)[2]	Revised weighting	
Criminal supervision		*Time in minutes*		
1. Probation	90	120	120	
2. C&YP supervision	90	105	120	[3]
3. MPS	60	20	30	
4. SSS	-	70	75	[4]

---

[1] NAPO weighting excludes all travelling and some recording time.

[2] NARS includes all recording but no travelling. Figures have been rounded to the nearest 5.

[3] Ought to equate with probation.

[4] Clearly less time consuming than probation.

122

Supervision	Present NAPO weighting	NARS finding (rounded)	Revised weighting	
After care		*Time in minutes*		
5. Life licence: pre-release	180	55	60	
6. Life licence: post release	180	55	120	5
7. Parole: pre-release	180	75	60	
8. Parole: post-release	180	120	120	6
9. Other statutory pre-release	-	80	60	
10. Other statutory post-release	-	75	120	7
11. Voluntary pre-release	60	55	60	8
12. Voluntary post-release	90	50	60	9
Civil supervision				
13. Matrimonial & wardship: 1 child	60	65	60	
14. More than 1 child	45	55	60	10
15. Matrimonial conciliation	240	110	120	11

---

[5] Equate with parole.

[6] Equate with probation.

[7] Equate with probation.

[8] Considerable pre-release investment.

[9] Generally low key focus

[10] Weighting per child should be the same whether one or several children in the family.

[11] To be counted only if case seen during that month.

Inquiry work:	Present NAPO weighting	NARS finding (rounded)	Revised weighting	[12]
		Time in minutes		
16. Magistrates: adults	240	135	180	[13]
17. Magistrates: juveniles	240	130	180	
18. Crown Court	240	145	180	
19. Means Inquiry	120	130	120	[14]
20. Home circumstance report	–	55	60	[15]
Civil reports				
21. Family Division & County Court: shared	600	320	360	[16]
22. " " : sole	600	510	600	
23. Matrimonial Proceedings Inquiry: shared	480	345	360	[17]
24. Matrimonial Proceedings Inquiry: sole	480	670	600	
25. Guardian ad litem (GAL): adoption	420	295	360	
26. GAL: Children Act 1975	–	250	360	
27. GAL: Custodianship	–	–	360	

---

[12] Re. NAPO and NARS, all figures include recording time but exclude travelling time.

[13] NARS clearly indicates that time for 1 SIR (SER) should not be twice that for a probation order.

[14] NAPO weighting retaines as NARS sample small.

[15] Subject already known as pre-release after-care. Chief need would be for recommendation.

[16] Ought to be more than half a sole report.

[17] May be as difficult and time consuming as divorce inquiry.

These 'provisionally agreed' weightings for SERs (SIRs) were disputed by NAPO who argued in a letter to chief probation officers that 'good professional practice' required the retention of the original 1972 weighting. A compromise of 3.5 units was offered (1 unit equating with 1 hour), this was still unacceptable to NAPO, but the revision stood- the allocation for SERs was 3.5 units (210 minutes).

References

Algie, J. (1971), 'Allocating Scarce Resources' in *British Hospital Journal*, February.

Algie, J. & C. Miller, (1976), 'Deciding social services priorities' Part 1 & in *Social Work Today*, vol 6 nos 22 & 23.

Algie, J. (1981), *Social Values, Objectives and Action*, Kogan Page, London.

Audit Commission (1986), *Making a Reality of Community Care*, HMSO, London.

Audit Commission (1989), *The Probation Service: Promoting Value for Money*, HMSO, London.

Avison, D. & A.T. Wood-Harper (1992), *Multiview*, Alfred Waller, Henley on Thames.

Barclay, P. M. (1982), *Social Workers: their Role and Tasks*, Bedford Square Press, London.

BASW (1977), *The Social Work Task*, British Association of Social Work, Birmingham.

Bateson, G. (1970), *Steps to an Ecology of Mind*, Ballantine, New York.

Beaumont, B. (1986), 'Watch Those Hours' in *NAPO Newsletter* no 259, NAPO, London.

Bottoms, A. & A. Stelman (1988), *Social Inquiry Reports*, Wildwood House, Aldershot.

Buckle, J. (1981), *Intake Teams*, Tavistock, London.

Carver, V. & J.L. Edwards, (1972), *Social Workers and their Workloads*, NISW, London.

CCETSW (1991), *DipSW Rules and Requirements for the Diploma of Social*

Work Paper 30 (second edition), Central Council of Education and Training, London.

Cherniss, G. (1980), *Staff Burnout: Job Stress in the Human Services*, Sage, New York.

Colombi, D. (1994), *The Probation Service and Information Technology*, Avebury in association with CEDR, Aldershot.

Coulshed, V. (1989), *Social Work Practice*, BASW/Macmillan, Basingstoke.

Coulshed, V. (1990), *Management in Social Work*, BASW/Macmillan Basingstoke.

Crawforth, J. (1987), 'Efficiency and Effectiveness: FMIS and the Deployment of Resources' in *Research, Information and Practice in the Probation Service*, proceedings of the Third Sheffield Conference organised by NIPRIE, University of Sheffield and Midlands Regional Staff Development Office.

Curnock, K. & P. Hardiker (1979), *Towards a Practice Theory: Skills and Methods in Social Assessment*, RKP, London.

Croft, S. & P. Beresford (1986), *Whose Welfare: Private Care of Public Services?* L. Cohen Urban Studies Centre, Brighton.

Davies, M. & A. Knopf (1973), *Social Inquiry Reports and the Probation Service*, Home Office Research Unit Report, 18, HMSO, London.

Davies P., Dyson P., Lynch G. & C. Miller (1988), 'Workloads and Resources' in *Social Work Today*.

Davies P., Dyson P., Lynch G. & C. Miller (1988), 'Bottom Up Top Down Planning' in Community Care 13 October, pp22-3.

Dews, V. (1995) *Review of Education and Training for the Probation Service*, Home Office, London.

Everitt, A., Hardiker, P., Littlewood, J & A. Mullender (1992), *Applied Research for Better Practice*, BASW/Macmillan, Basingstoke.

Farendon, J. (1987), 'Financial Information Systems and the Probation Service' in *Research, Information and Practice in the Probation Service* Proceedings of the Third Sheffield Conference organised by NIPRIE, University of Sheffield and Midlands Regional Staff Development Office.

Ford, P., Orme, J. & S. Sleeman (1993), 'Translating Agreements between Partners into effective delivery of Probation streams, in *Developing Guidance for DipSW programmes with probation streams* CCETSW, London.

Foucault, M. (1977), *Discipline and Punishment* Allen & Lane, London.

Glastonbury, B. (1979), *Paying the Piper and Calling the Tune: being a study of public attitudes towards social work*, BASW, Southampton.

Glastonbury, B. Bradley, R. and J. Orme, (1987), *Managing People in the Personal Social Services*, Wiley, Chichester.

Godson, D. & C. McConnell, (1989), *Social Enquiry Reports - Practice and Policy in Hampshire*, Research and Information Unit, Hampshire Probation Service, Winchester.

Goldberg, E.M. (1972), 'The Use of Research in Social Work Education' in *New Themes in Social Work Education* International Association of Schools of Social Work, New York.

Goldberg, E.M. & D.J. Fruin (1976), 'Towards Accountability in Social Work' in the *British Journal of Social Work* 6,1 pp4-22.

Griffiths Report (1988), *Community Care: Agenda for Action*, London, HMSO,

Hadley, R. & M. McGrath (1980), *Going Local: neighbourhood social services*, National Council for Voluntary Organisations, London.

Hampshire Probation Service (1994), *Targeting Matrix: A guide to stuctured decion-making for practitioners*, Winchester.

Home Office (1983a), *Social Inquiry Reports: General Guidance on Contents* Home Office Circular 17/1983, HMSO, London.

Home Office (1983b), *Social Inquiry Reports: Recommendations Relevant to Sentencing*, Home Office Circular 18/1983, HMSO, London.

Home Office (1984), *The Statement of National Objectives and Priorities for the Probation Service in England and Wales*, HMSO, London.

Home Office (1986), *Social Inquiry Reports*, Home Office Circular 92/1986, HMSO, London.

Home Office (1988), *Performance Indicators for the Probation Service*, a report by the HM Inspectorate of Probation, HMSO, London.

Home Office (1989), *Determine Information to be produced by FMIS: Second Report from the FMIS Project Team*, HMSO, London.

Home Office (1989a) *Resource Management Information Systems*, Stage 3a, HMSO, London.

Home Office (1989b), *A Financial Management Information System for Area Probation Services: Stage 3A Draft Functional Requirements Specification*, HMSO, London.

Home Office (1990), *Managing RMIS in Practice*, HMSO, London.

Home Office (1990a), *A Probation Service Financial Information Service* paper prepared by the Home Office for consideration by the Central Council of Probation Committees, the Association of Chief Officers of Probation, and the National Association of Probation Officers.

Home Office (1990b), *Supervision and Punishment in the Community: A framework for action* HMSO, London.

Home Office (1990c), *Probation Statistics for England and Wales for 1989*, HMSO, London.

Home Office (1992), *National Standards for the Supervision of Offenders in the Community* HMSO, London.

Home Office (1992), *Partnership in Dealing with Offenders in the Community*, HMSO, London.

Home Office (1993), *Case Records and Administration System Requirements and Evaluation Study*, Probation Service Division, ISSU, London.

Home Office (1993a), CPO33/1993 *Letter to Chief Probation Officers from the Home Office*, London.

Home Office (1994), *The Probation Service National Case Records System - CRAMS- Overview*, HMSO, London.

Home Office (1994a) *The Quality and Provision of Expedited Pre-Sentence*

Reports Prepared for the Crown Court by the Probation Service HM Inspectorate of the Probation Service, London

Home Office (1995), *Strengthening Punishment in the Community: a Consultation Document*, HMSO Cm 2780, London.

Killeen, C. (1986), 'Workload management' in *NAPO Newsletter* no 260 p6 November .

Knapp, M. (1984), *The Economics of Social Care*, Macmillan, Basingstoke.

Lloyd-Owen, D. (1977), in *The Practice of Supervision in Social Work: A Guide for Staff Supervisors* (ed) Westheimer, I.J., Wary Lock, London.

May, C. (1992), *The National Probation Survey 1990*, Home Office Research and Planning Unit Paper 72, HMSO, London.

McDonald, G. (1994), 'Developing Empirically-based Practice in Probation' in *British Journal of Social Work*, **24** 4 pp405-428.

McWilliams, B. (1990), 'Probation Practice and the Management Ideal' in *Probation Journal* **37** 2 pp60-67.

NAPO (1972), *Workloads in the Probation and After Care Service*, National Association of Probation Officers, London.

NAPO (1979), *Probation Service Workload Measure - Revised Version*, National Association of Probation Officers, London.

NAPO (1989), *A Probation Service Resource Management Information System: A NAPO View*.

NAPO (1989a), *Information Strategy - towards a NAPO perspective*.

NAPO (1990), *NAPO's Response to "Managing RMIS into Practice"*.

NAPO (1991), *Value for Money Information Strategies* draft statement of the Professional Committee.

NAPO (1992), *Proposed Workload Limitation Scheme for the Probation Service* Professional Committee.

NAPO (1995), 'Workload Limitation' in NAPO News no 68, NAPO, London.

NAPO (1995b), *Good Practice Guide* NAPO, London.

Oldfield, M (1994), 'The McDonaldisation of the Probation Service' in *Probation Journal*, **41** 4 pp186-192.

O'Hagan, K. (1986), *Crisis Intervention in Social Services*, BASW/Macmillan, Basingstoke.

Orme, J. (1989), 'Can Workloads Be Measured' in *Probation Journal* vol 35 no 2, pp57-9.

Orme, J. (1989a), Diary Exercise of tasks/workloads in the Probation Service (unpublished).

Orme, J. & I. Forbes (1991), 'Equal Opportunities in Higher Degree Research' in *Handbook for Research Students in Social Sciences* (ed) Allan, G. & C. Skinner, Falmer Press, London

Orme, J. & B. Glastonbury (1993), *Care Management: tasks and workloads* BASW/Macmillan, Basingstoke.

Orme, J. (1995), 'Social Work Education: reactive or proactice?' in *Social Work Education: State of the Art*, official congress publication of 27th

Congress of IASSW, Hogeschool van Amsterdam, July 1994 pp 127-136.

Osmond R., Missing R., Tunstall V. & R. Lewry (1977), 'The Caseload Monitoring System' in *Social Work Today*, **8**, No 16.

Parker, R.A. (1967), 'Social Administration and Scarcity: the problems of rationing' in *Social Work*, April.

Parsloe, P. (1981), *Social Services Area Teams*, Allen and Unwin, London.

Parton, N (1994), 'Problematics of Government', (Post) Modernity and Social Work' in *British Journal of Social Work* **24**, pp9-32.

Payne, R.L. (1979), 'Demands, supports, constraints and psychological health', in Payne, R.L. (ed.), *Response to Stress: Occupational Aspects* IPC.

Powell, J. & R. Lovelock (1992), *Changing Patterns of Mental Health Care*, Avebury in conjunction with CEDR, Aldershot.

Prime, R. (1977), 'Report on a method of workload management and weighting' in *Social Work Today*, **9**, No 15.

Pritchard, C. (1985), *Maintaining Morale through Staff Development and Training*, Social Work Monographs 40, UEA, Norwich.

Raynor, P. (1980), 'Is there any sense in Social Inquiry reports?' in *Probation Journal*, **27** 3 pp 78-84.

Raynor, P. (1984), 'Evaluation with One Eye Closed: The Empiricist Agenda, in Social Work Research' in *British Journal of Social Work* **14**, pp1-10.

Raynor, P. (1988), *Probation as an Alternative to Custody: A Case Study* Avebury, Aldershot.

Reid, W.J. & L. Epstein (1972), *Task Centred Casework*, Columbia University Press, Columbia.

Ross, S. & A. Bilson (1989), *Social Work Management and Practice: systems principles*, Jessica Kingsley Publishers, London.

Sainsbury, E. (1970), *Social Diagnosis in Casework*, RKP, 1970.

Sheldon, B. (1983), 'The Use of Single Case Experimental Design in the Evaluation of Social Work' in *British Journal of Social Work* **13**, 477-500.

Stanley, L (1990), '"A referral was made": behind the scenes during the creation of a Social Services Department 'elderly' statistic' in (ed) Stanley, L. *Feminist Praxis*, Routledge, London.

Shepherd, G. (1990), 'Management: Short of Ideals?' in *Probation Journal*, **37** no 4 pp 176-181.

Thorpe, J. & K.Pease (1976), 'The Relationship Between Recommendations Made to the Court and Sentences Passed' in *British Journal of Criminology*, 16(4), pp393-394.

Ungerson, C. (1987), *Policy is Personal*, Tavistock, London.

Vickery, A. (1977), *Caseload Management: a guide for supervisors of social work staff*, National Institute for Social Work Papers No 5, NISW, London.

Whitehead, P. (1990), *Management Information Systems in Probation* UEA Probation Monograph no 92, UEA, Norwich.